Assessment for Learning

Ruth Sutton

with illustrations by Jim Whittaker

RS Publications

Published by **RS Publications**
29 Nevile Court, Nevile Road,
Salford M7 3PS, England, UK
Telephone & Fax +44 (0)161 708 8880

Typeset by The Mac Base, Kirkham, Lancs

Printed and bound in Great Britain by
John Roberts & Sons Printers (Salford) Ltd
Chapel Street, Salford

ISBN 0 9523871 1 5

Contents

Acknowledgements

Thanks yet again are due to the rest of the small team which has produced this book following on the success of 'School Self Review' in 1994. Jim Whittaker provided some more of his splendid cartoons, I have tapped away into my faithful laptop, and Mary McSherry, as ever, has done everything else.

I also want to thank the thousands of teachers whose experience, ideas and common sense have sharpened my thoughts since I last wrote at length about assessment. After thirteen years of working on assessment issues in ever more varied contexts I still find them fascinating; a combination of technical, philosophical, management and political questions. More important than all that, assessment **matters** because it fundamentally affects our children's experience at school, and beyond.

Introduction

This book is designed to complement *Assessment: A Framework for Teachers* which I wrote in 1991. That book was a starter: this one is a little more like the main course, still digestible I hope, but going a little deeper into some aspects of assessment for learning which were introduced before.

The recipe is much the same as before. The ingredients are ideas and suggestions relevant to teachers and schools in the United Kingdom and beyond. I've tried to use plain language for clarity, and to include terminology from the Antipodes and North America to make it travel better. Every now and then you'll find a section in italics: this usually denotes a 'story', to exemplify or supplement the ideas in the main text. Towards the end of each chapter you'll find a summary of key points, and these are all listed again at the end, for those of you who like to start at the back. Reading the whole book shouldn't take you more than a couple of hours: acting upon some of its suggestions might take a little longer. As you read, you will notice that I've used female and male pronouns alternately, rather than using one gender all the time or resorting to he/she and her/his. Take it as a 'statement' if you wish: I was trying to make it sound more fluent.

Above all, my aim is to communicate some of the central questions in education which emerge as we consider assessment. These questions are not necessarily technical or statistical, nor are they

The Planning, learning and assessment cycle

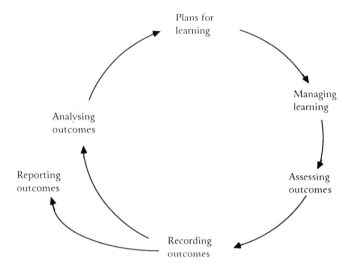

easily answered, but we still need to debate them, not just among educators but in the wider community. You will find one of these 'big questions' at the end of each chapter.

The central theme is the interconnection between planning and assessment in the learning process. This very basic representation of the process serves to remind us that it is cyclical, not linear. Wherever you break the cycle to examine the component parts in greater depth you end up having to go all the way round or all the way back. **The stages around the cycle must be consistent with each other.** Let's start with planning.

Chapter One:
Planning

Teaching is about communicating in order to enable others to learn. The activity can take a wide variety of forms, but it is not usually totally unplanned and spontaneous. The teacher has some aim in mind: she may start from the existing knowledge and curiosity of the learner, or from a set of things she wants the learner to learn, or from a list of requirements established by others. In any event, she has a plan. It may be in her head, or it may be written down, but it exists.

> *A teacher I knew once seemed to defy this assumption, particularly with the younger secondary pupils he taught, whom he was less interested in. He entered the room. He spoke to the class. "Who are you?" They chorused their response. "What did we do last week?" He pointed at a likely bright face and gained some reply. "Right" he said, and away he went, drawing not on a specifically prepared plan but on twenty years' experience which instantly provided him with sufficient to mould a 40–minute lesson. He was funny and knowledgeable and on a good day the children were spellbound. It was not the best model of professional practice for a young teacher like myself, but it worked sometimes. He had a plan, in fact he had quite a few to choose from: the choice depended on the answers to his two questions.*

In this chapter about planning, I'm going to assume that teachers are not planning solely from the perceived needs of their pupils: they are required to take account of some prescription in the curriculum to be offered. In the United Kingdom, as a result of the 1988 Education Act, a National Curriculum is in place, to which all school pupils are entitled.

When the model was first developed this entitlement was so specific and wide-ranging that it swallowed up all available teaching time, although this had not apparently been the intention. After much tribulation and waste of energy the entitlement was reduced to more manageable proportions, but it still dominates much of the curriculum planning process. The idea of a National Curriculum can now be found in all parts of the globe, and is even mooted in federal systems like the USA and Australia, although individual states still exert the major influence there.

In England and Wales, the National Curriculum is laid down in various learning areas, Maths, History, Physical Education, and so on. It is also divided into Key Stages, reflecting the age-related stages in the child's experience at school. Key Stage One covers the time between the child's fifth birthday and the end of Year 2, Key Stage Two from Year 3 to Year 6 and Key Stage Three from Year 7 to Year 9. 'Programmes of Study' are laid down for each learning area and for each Key Stage. These are the statutory entitlement, and have to be taken into account in a school's curriculum plans.

The best advice when dealing with any prescribed curriculum is not to treat it as a **teaching** programme, but to consider your existing curriculum first and compare it with the prescribed curriculum, looking for match and mismatch between the two and planning to improve the match by a well-managed evolution over a reasonable period of time. There would be little benefit to children in bringing in 'new' topics, content and skills without the necessary development of teachers' expertise and resources.

A further necessary step in effective planning of both teaching and assessment is to take time together to consider the **big picture**, to establish what will be the curriculum experience of the child as she or he moves through the school, from one class to the next. In the secondary school the pupil moves not only from year to year but also constantly from subject specialist to specialist. This presents a double challenge to the organisation of learning in the secondary school, to which we shall return later.

For the time being, we'll look at the 'big picture' which needs to be developed in the primary (or intermediate) school, where the class teacher provides most if not all the learning for her pupils.

What is meant by the 'big picture'?

This is the outline of the overall teaching experiences offered within the key stage or the school. It could be achieved in either of two ways, both of which require big sheets of paper to encompass the key elements of learning which progress year by year as the child moves up the school. Visual presentation of the information is vital if we are to see connections and recognise trends: these are much harder to spot if we rely on sequential presentation either written or spoken. The best place for the 'diagrams with words'which we are trying to create is a wall in the staff room when everyone concerned can absorb the information simultaneously.

Vertical threads

In one model, the school's existing curriculum is 'mapped' topic by topic, with the main objectives of each topic being added, and the ongoing threads of skills and learning areas perhaps being identified using colour or other symbols. The alternative method is to map each learning/subject area separately and focus on key objectives in these first, adding the context (that is, the activities in the topic) later. In this method, we would probably start with, say, Maths or Writing and plot the spiral of experiences and expectations onto your map, adding in more learning areas one at a time. It's important to focus on the underpinning learning objectives rather than just the content to be taught. Some 'facts' are going to be taught of course, but sometimes too the content is just the context within which we explore more fundamental concepts skills or values.

> *The school staff were looking together at the whole curriculum offering. They discovered that the children were studying tadpoles almost annually: certainly tadpoles figured quite large in the curriculum in Year 2, Year 3 and Year 6. An argument began to bubble about who should continue to 'do tadpoles' and who should not. Soon they realised that what was important were the reasons why they were 'doing tadpoles', and this produced different objectives in the three different year groups. Once they had*

established this, the discussion moved on to how best to use the study of tadpoles to learn and develop certain scientific skills and concepts at progressive levels of sophistication, or how to use it a springboard into a different approach, as a stimulus for writing for example.

Having established together what the overview looks like, it should now be possible to compare current provision with the national, state or local entitlement. We identify the 'match' between what we already do and what is required of us, and realise that the 'new' curriculum is not completely new and therefore less of a problem. We can also identify 'mismatch', the gaps between what is required and our existing provision, gaps which will eventually have to be filled to ensure that the children all receive their entitlement. These gaps, where they occur, will be addressed in our three-year curriculum development plan, managing the change step by step to make sure that we're not just plugging the gap for the sake of it.

Horizontal slices

In all but the very smallest schools, children are usually arranged in age-related classes for teaching purposes, at least in the English-speaking systems I am most familiar with. A teacher often specialises in teaching a particular age group, and may be less familiar with the actual learning activities experienced by the children both before they arrive and after they leave her. When the teachers look together at the big picture, they regain the sense that each teacher is making a **contribution** to the overall learning of the child. To define more clearly the precise nature of that contribution, we now take the big picture and slice it horizontally, to reflect the experience of a child over a single year, or over two or more years in a mixed age class. For each slice, we discuss and record the learning experiences and expectations for our children. What learning opportunities do we offer to children

7

at each stage? What do we hope that they will **all** achieve, and what beyond that would we be aiming for with **some?**

This is your first step towards **differentiation** in your curriculum plan. The whole of Chapter Two is devoted to unpicking this notion, but inevitably we've bumped into it already. Basically it's about our recognition of the differences among children which affect their learning, and which should therefore be catered for in our teaching. It's the hardest challenge the teacher faces because of the numbers of children we teach and the constraints of time, resources, and all the institutional features of schools, like timetables, bells, the size of rooms and so on. Each child is unique, but schools lump them together. On balance, schools may be the best way to provide education for all our children, but we recognise the compromise involved and keep trying to let the individual needs of individual children flourish in the collective environment.

Does the progressive sum of all these slices amount to the entitlement curriculum for all our pupils? At this early planning stage, can we ensure that our expectations and the challenge of our planned activities do progress over time? Can we avoid unnecessary repetition which sometimes happens when all teachers are not fully aware of what happens elsewhere round the school? Can we stretch the curriculum offering thin, so that we avoid having to go too fast for some children, and also avoid undermining the quality of our assessment by assessing too much too frequently?

The talk around the table during these stages of the planning process is vital. Apart from assisting progression, it is the first stage in sharing our interpretations of the prescribed curriculum and of the assessment criteria we shall all use later to gather information about children's learning. This talk is too important to be tackled at the end of a working day when everyone is tired and time is short. If you can find any way of giving yourselves some high-quality time to focus on the big picture it would be a worthwhile investment for the future.

The introduction of the revised National Curriculum gave the school opportunity and encouragement to look again together at the big picture of the curriculum. A 'teacher-only' or staff development day would have been ideal, but this was not available to the school for a variety of reasons. The Principal put the question to the trustees (i.e. the Governors). They agreed to allow the school day to start at 11 a.m. on a given day, making sure that parents had plenty of notice and a proper explanation of the reasons. The teachers agreed to begin the day with breakfast together at 7.30 a.m. and start their meeting at 8 a.m. Then they could work for two and a half hours, while they were fresh, and still have time to prepare for and welcome the children at 11 a.m. Their meeting was effective because the Staff Development Co-ordinator had worked with the Principal to make sure that the subject co-ordinators were well prepared to make their contribution, background documents were circulated in advance, big tables and paper were available to spread everything out on, and the Deputy was asked to use her skills to keep her colleagues going, on task, and ensure that they all had an opportunity to contribute. The outcomes of their efforts, when they had been tidied up, were shown to the trustees for their comment, and put on display in the entrance hall for a week so that parents could see what the overall curriculum plan looked like. The teachers felt that they achieved more by this strategy than they could have done with a whole term's worth of meetings after school. They realised that they couldn't use such a method regularly and looked again at the way they planned their training days to ensure that they were as effective as possible. Then

> *they could use the after–school meetings slot for matters which did not need such collective high-energy time.*

Some points for discussion while planning a 'chunk'

The next stage in the planning process involves teachers working on the particular slice of the school curriculum for which they are responsible. In larger schools, with parallel classes in year groups, this still means being able to work with someone else, in a pair at least. Even if a single teacher is responsible for the slice it's still helpful to liaise with someone, to share ideas and resources, to talk to about standards and expectations, to maximise the support for weaker or less experienced colleagues. For all sorts of reasons, which we shall keep on coming across, shared planning is a good idea.

The planning now moves from 'whole school' to single class, starting from the point where the teacher is clear about her overall intentions and needs for the year, which derive from a combination of the big picture for the school, the entitlement of the children and her own professional judgement. Towards that end she begins to design 'chunks' of learning, each with a particular purpose or focus. Alongside these she will run her continuing programmes for reading, and any other specific learning activities which are not incorporated into the more multi-disciplinary chunks. A chunk, by the way, is just a generic word covering a host of others like 'topic', 'module', 'unit', and so on. Most 'chunks' last for several days, or several class 'periods' depending on the structure of your teaching timetable.

While we're on terminology, i.e. the words we use to describe things, let's remind ourselves to use terms with care, and check that they mean the same things to all the people who use them. When describing teachers' plans we need words for three types of plan – long–term plans, covering a sweep of teaching intentions over a year or a key stage; medium–term plans, covering several days or class periods; and short–term plans, for a day, a particular activity, or a class period. All sorts of terms are used to describe these various plans.

Some terms, such as 'scheme of work' have been typically used at secondary level for long–term plans. The use of this term in the UK school inspection manual has caused some confusion in primary schools which had long–term plans but called them something else and began to worry about writing schemes of work. The primary school teacher, who will mostly work with the same group of children all day, will often have quite detailed notes to guide her over the course of a day and a week, whereas the secondary school teacher, who could see up to two hundred children in seven different groups over the course of a day will probably plan in a different way, to ensure the continuity of teaching from one meeting with a group to the next, which could be days later.

Essentially, it doesn't matter what we call these plans so long as all the people using the terms understand them consistently. This is particularly important when talking to people from other schools, and from other phases of the education service. Effective discussion between primary and secondary teachers can be badly undermined by the use of language which means something to you but nothing at all or something completely different to others.

The 'loose/ tight' dilemma in planning

All of us would agree that good schools have a sense of purpose and direction in the curriculum they offer children. As the children pass from one teacher to another, either 'vertically' (from one year to the next) or 'horizontally' (from one class period to the next during the day), or both, we hope that they will connect and build their learning progressively, rather than experience a series of unconnected bits and pieces.

No teacher is an island, despite the very architecture of most schools which creates 'egg box' structures, dividing teacher from teacher with walls. Teaching has been described as the second most private adult activity, and some of us go to considerable lengths to pursue that privacy, covering over the glass in the door, or constructing walls where none exist, using shelves and cabinets and screens and any other materials we can find.

There are some tensions here which affect our approach to planning so fundamentally that we need to explore them for a while. Let's start by looking at the needs of the children, or any learners come to that. On the one hand, learners have a right to expect that the teaching offered to them has been considered beforehand, so that the necessary 'kit' is available, that activities start and finish on time, that we all know what is the point or purpose of what we're being asked to do, and that we have a rough idea what's going to happen next. On the other hand, if the plan is too tight and rigid there may be no flexibility at all – to spend more time on something really interesting, to go over something which isn't clear, to connect what we're learning with other things going around us, or with what we already know about.

All these learning considerations matter to teachers too. Experience, and sometimes an intuition teachers may be blessed with, recognises the 'teachable moment' and is able to make use of it. Often these moments occur with individuals, and surprise us. Sometimes a whole class or group suddenly clicks and takes off in a particular direction which you may not have planned for but you can make use of, if only to capture the prevailing interest and build the motivation of the group. But you can't teach effectively every day by just waiting for the teachable moment, or at least I can't !

So here we are looking at the loose/tight dilemma in planning, and teaching too. Too tight, and teaching can't respond to those unanticipated things which give it life and energy: too loose and we drift aimlessly, making huge demands on our concentration in class to respond to everything that crops up, and ignoring the expectations of other teachers, parents or any 'prescribed' curriculum or syllabus. Obviously we make choices which lie somewhere these two extremes.

These choices are affected by all sorts of considerations:

- a personal preference for order and structure in our lives or a more open-ended and spontaneous approach;

- the demands of the organisation or team in which we work;

- the nature of the particular chunk of learning we are presenting. Some learning needs very careful, step by step, management to ensure it is effective, while other aspects lend themselves to more open-ended treatment;

- concern for 'coverage', to make sure through specific tight planning and teaching that we cover all the ground, which is usually prescribed by others;

- concern about 'accountability', so that we can prove our intention to teach in a way expected by those we feel accountable to;

- our awareness of preferences among our pupils for working in a particular way. Some learners thrive on tight sequential approaches while others want more freedom to experiment, and teachers can recognise and respond to these preferences if they wish.

Clearly, within this list of considerations, concerns about coverage and accountability will probably make planning tighter, if they are allowed to predominate over the other more intrinsic reasons. This may explain a phenomenon I have witnessed as the external inspection of schools has been introduced in some systems alongside a more prescribed curriculum framework. This could be described as the 'pre-inspection tighten up and laminate your plans syndrome'. Teachers' plans may be the first things the inspectors actually see, and we feel they ought to look good, and demonstrate our intention to 'cover' what we are supposed to be covering. Even if the teachers are unconvinced about this, the Headteacher may insist that certain 'cosmetic' standards are reached in the presentation of plans. For teachers whose planning had become too loose, this may be a salutary exercise, but in some cases this tightening can have a damaging effect on what happens in the classroom.

Our teaching plans are now more detailed, more structured, more tidy and visually attractive than before, and it's taken hours of our time to make them so. Now the plan goes into practice. Because life and children are not entirely predictable, it may soon be clear that learning is not taking place for some or all of the children as you hoped and planned that it would. Now there's a dilemma: do you depart from the plan to pursue the actual learning of the pupils, or do you stick to the plan in which you have invested so much energy, and expect the pupils to cope, or catch up, or stop asking awkward questions? If – heaven forbid – the plan is laminated, you're even more stuck, when you discover that you can't alter a laminated plan. You have to make a choice based on balance of need between teaching and learning. Don't forget, you can teach till you're exhausted but learning won't necessarily take place. Even if you do 'cover' everything in your plan, what's the point if the pupils haven't learned it? The curriculum is not what teachers put into it, but what the learners take away with them. We know all this, but sometimes we make the easy choice when we're under pressure, not the right choice.

So here is the ultimate irony. An inspection process and a national curriculum framework can, **if we let them**, have an

impact on our teaching which may make learning less effective in our schools.

These issues are worth discussing among yourselves, and with your school governors or trustees who may be ultimately responsible for the delivery of the curriculum. We need to clarify our terms, weigh the pros and cons of various approaches to planning, and make some sensible decisions about the loose/tight dilemma. For example:

- by looking at the big picture we recognise how we achieve coverage over the longer term but still avoid overcrowding of the curriculum in the medium or short term;

- we leave some space in every medium–term plan, to allow for the unexpected, to give time for remediation or consolidation if necessary, to enable challenging extension work to be offered to those learners who need it, to have some fun with a related but less essential aspect of the topic, to tackle something from a completely different perspective. The amount of space we could leave might not be much, an hour or two during the second half of a twelve–hour chunk maybe, after we've done enough to see what the needs are. It gives us the opportunity to customise the plan without jeopardising it.

- the timing of assessment within a chunk allows for the outcomes of the assessment to be followed up within the chunk itself, rather than having to be postponed to the next relevant opportunity;

- we try to find out what degree of structure best suits different children in the class, and offer them different approaches to the same task;

- we build alternatives or choices into the plan itself, to balance structure and flexibility;

- we give ourselves more structure when we're less sure of our ground, or less experienced in this particular aspect, then loosen up when we have the confidence to do so successfully. This may mean that we may not recognise or respond to the 'teachable moment' for a while, knowing that we will be able to do so when we're more sure. It's hard to 'take off' when you're only a few pages ahead of the children ! If you're very anxious, or tired, or unwell, or upset about something, it's hard to recognise and respond to what the children are doing, so you lean on a tighter than normal plan to see you through.

I don't teach children any more, but I do a lot of in-service training, which is a form of teaching. When I first started training on assessment issues, responding to questions was hard because I wasn't familiar enough with all the issues and their implications. It was tempting to dodge the hard questions and just keep going, to stay in charge and make sure I got through the things I'd planned to do. As my own understanding and experience grew I found I was listening more carefully to what teachers said to me and asked about, because I was better able to respond and to connect the response with the broader picture now in my head. By listening better I learned more, made more connections, and sustained my own interest. I wish I could believe that about my time in the classroom.

Planning a chunk

Now, at long last, we come around to the basic building block of the curriculum – the actual activities we design for pupils, related to a particular set of learning objectives. I've left this until now because it helps to think about the big picture and the loose/tight fit before you embark on this step. Many schools now have clear guidelines for planning, and some even have a uniform format for all teachers' plans. All I'm going to offer here are what these guidelines or formats need to address.

- **Connections** with previous learning experiences and outcomes. If we're not sure about this, how do we find out? How shall we help the pupils to make those connections?

- Clear **objectives** for learning, derived from the combination of the big picture, the prescribed curriculum and your professional judgement about the child or the group, and their needs as you see them.

- Learning **outcomes** – a more specific description of what it would look/sound like if these learning objectives were being achieved. You may find you don't need both objectives and outcomes, but you definitely need a pretty clear and specific picture of what you want the pupils to achieve, whatever heading you use for it.

- The steps you will take to ensure that every child can get access to the activity, in terms of the instructions given, the time allowed, the reading age of written materials, the learning style involved, and so on. These are the key steps towards effective differentiation, to be pursued in more depth later on.

- The materials and **resources** needed, suited to the pupils and relevant to your objectives. This might include decisions about the layout of the room, the size and composition of groups within the class, the time to be given to various aspects, the booking of a scarce resource like the video, or the drama studio/hall, or a visiting speaker.

- The **assessment** approach: this would include your assessment objectives, the criteria to be looked for, decisions about who is the appropriate person to do the assessment and by what methods. The learning objectives/outcomes you have described earlier provide you with opportunities for assessment, but you would not need to use all these opportunities. The knack in assessment is to **focus** and gather revealing and useful information: **go for quality not quantity**.

- What **records** you will need to keep, to capture the outcomes of the assessment on paper or on disc so that you don't have to rely entirely on memory. Obviously you can't keep a record of everything that happens for every child all the time, so you'll have to decide what are the significant outcomes, what record structure would best accommodate these, who is the most appropriate person to do the record-keeping, who the records are for and how they are to be used.

- Will the activity produce any **outcomes** for all or some children which you might want **to keep and refer to later?** If so, would it be helpful to have some written items on paper rather than in books? Would a camera be useful, or a video? We have neither the time nor the resources in most schools to use technology regularly to preserve the more ephemeral outcomes of pupils' learning, and if we want to do so we will have to plan ahead.

- Connect the outcomes of this topic with targets or expectations for the future, and share this **'feedforward'** with the pupils. Try to act upon some of this feedforward immediately, to reinforce it and produce some immediate improvement in the work, but in any case identify a target or two, for some of the pupils and/or the whole group and make sure these are recorded somewhere so that they are remembered and can be referred to later. This loops back to the first item in our list, and the planning, teaching, learning cycle is completed.

- The ways in which the **pupils** themselves could and should be **involved** with any of the aspects mentioned already. This involvement might be in adding details of the activity to the outline you present to them at the start. Or they could help you manage the materials and resources the activity might need, leaving you with more time to guide, observe, listen. With help and clear criteria, they might learn to assess some aspects of their own or each other's learning, or keep track of some of their own experiences, learning and targets for the future. The whole of Chapter Seven is devoted to student involvement.

Involving the pupils does not mean that the teacher abandons her professional responsibility, accountability or control over the learning environment, so don't be put off by any simplistic arguments over this. The teacher's job is to produce learning in her pupils: if involving the pupils produces such learning more efficiently than not doing so, we do it. There will be times, for a host of reasons, when you need to say to a group, "I'm in charge now, and we're going to do it this way." It's like the decisions about the tightness of your planning structure: you weigh up what a particular set of circumstances need and make the best judgement at the time. If anyone asked you why you had decided to do whatever you're doing, you would be able to tell them, even though the original decision had been almost intuitive and made very quickly. Really effective teachers will make decisions like these many times a day, based on intuition or experience or both. I'm spelling out the considerations because not all of us are blessed with intuition, and experience takes many years to accumulate.

Key points

1. **Start the curriculum planning process with a shared view of the 'big picture', for the whole school or for a 'key stage'.**

2. **Find an acceptable balance between the 'tight' plan, which may not be responsive to children's needs, and the 'loose' plan which lacks any sense of direction.**

3. **Deciding on learning objectives and expected learning outcomes is an essential part of planning for assessment.**

4. Share these objectives and expectations with your
   pupils.

One big question:

When does curriculum entitlement become curriculum prescription?

Chapter Two:
Differentiation

Over the past several years in the UK education service the term 'differentiation' has been commonly used, while still managing to retain its mystery. Schools' inspection reports all make reference to it, people write books about it and attend courses about it. But what is it? Why is it so hard to bring about? Is it something new, or merely one word to describe something we already know about? Is it just one more thing for teachers to feel guilty about?

Here's a simple definition, with apologies to those of you for whom such simplicity is unnecessary.

Differentiation is giving the right learning tasks to the right pupils. To achieve this we need to:

- recognise that each of our pupils is unique;

- gather accurate information about what each pupil can and can't do, and what they need in order to learn;

- design activities for pupils which take account of these starting points and learning needs;

- present these activities to pupils in such a way that each pupil is given learning targets within his/her **extended grasp.**

The dictionary may tell us that differentiation is about 'discriminating' or identifying differences, but in education it is more than that. It is about identifying differences which affect learning, and then using this knowledge to improve our teaching.

None of us would disagree with any of this, but the implications are challenging to say the least. However much we believe in the uniqueness of each child, we may doubt our ability – given the number of children we teach – to design individual learning programmes for each child. Such plans are expected, and even required by the Special Needs Code of Practice in England and Wales, for children with identified special learning needs, but this may not be achievable for all. The primary school teacher, who is with her group of children for most of the time, has more chance to get to know them and their learning needs, but has a formidable range of learning areas to cover. The secondary school teacher has a more restricted range of subject matter, but may see scores of children in any one week or timetable cycle.

An experienced secondary colleague of mine teaches Physical Education to over two hundred children in the course of a single day. Her first task is to remember

all the children's names. Then she has to find out and remember their particular strengths, talents and needs. Experience will have helped her to gather a wide range of teaching approaches from which to select the right approach for the right child, but she still feels that effective differentiation as we have defined it is beyond her extended grasp, and she has to come to terms with that without guilt. All she can do is her best, which she does.

Some of the experienced and talented teachers I work with tell me that the National Curriculum framework seems to make differentiation more difficult, by increasing the content that must be taught and reducing the teacher's freedom to match learning to the child's needs. We all hope that the looser and more concise framework of the revised National Curriculum will ease the problem somewhat.

Differentiation and school structures

As well as challenging the energy and organisational skills of individual teachers, differentiation also questions the assumptions we make about the learner's age. It may be possible to plot age in months and years against expected or 'average' attainment at that age, but the neat graphs which result are only the crudest indicator of expectations and in no way take account of the uniqueness of each learner. And yet in most schools pupils are taught in age-related year groups, leaving us to make important decisions about how we sub-divide the cohort.

As secondary schools are bigger generally than primary schools, this subdivision is more common. It can be done in order to make each subset reflect the full attainment range seen in the whole cohort, leading to 'mixed-ability' groups. Or it can be done to place children in a more homogeneous group relative to the criteria which are applied. This might result in 'streaming', where children are divided by some overall measure of 'ability' and taught in the same group for all subject areas. More commonly, it is recognised that 'ability' may vary from subject area to subject area, and children are 'setted' differently for different subjects. In some schools, children may be 'banded' into two or three broad overall ability bands, and then by 'mixed ability' within each band. Debate about these various structures is often heated and prolonged, but whichever grouping structure is adopted, the resulting groups remains 'mixed' because they contain as many learning needs as there are pupils. **Differentiation by ability group is not enough, even when the criteria for selection are both valid (accurate and relevant) and reliable (consistently applied). If the selection process lacks validity and reliability, differentiation by ability group is ineffective, inefficient and unfair.**

If we wished to take streaming, or more probably setting, to its logical conclusion we would go for mixed–age classes, and teach to the 'ability' not the age. The fact that schools don't normally do this, at least in the systems I know, recognises the social factors involved in teaching, and the impact of the learners' maturity, both physical and emotional, on their learning. All of us can recall instances when children have been taken out of their age peer group to be taught, but these are definitely exceptions, and sometimes controversial.

Differentiation by task and by outcome

Differentiation by task means that the teacher decides, based on her evidence, which children will get which task. This may work well, if the teacher's available evidence is accurate and relevant. If it is not so, the child may be given the wrong task, and may also begin to base part of his/her self-concept on the teacher's decision, and rise or fall to the level of that perceived expectation, making the original error quite hard to spot.

Differentiation by outcome means that the teacher offers the same learning experience to all the pupils, and uses the outcomes of the child's learning from this task to determine the differences she needs to be aware of. This is fine too, so long as the task itself actually allows each child to show what he or she knows and can do. If the task is properly to challenge the faster or higher attaining pupils it may look impossibly difficult to the slower or lower attaining pupils, who then do not show what they know because they are distracted by what they don't know. If on the other hand the task looks too pedestrian, the higher attaining pupil may be bored by it, not make a real effort, or skip over to a conclusion without demonstrating the reasons for that conclusion which the teacher needs to see. These design difficulties mean that even in mixed ability groups, effective teaching probably differentiates by task to some degree.

The key to effective differentiation therefore is the accuracy and relevance of the information we use to decide appropriate learning tasks for pupils, and our willingness to challenge these decisions from time to time by allowing pupils to surprise us. Even when most classroom differentiation may be by task, it's always possible to add the occasional planned opportunity to differentiate by outcome. This could be done at the end of a project or assessment task by asking pupils to speculate: "What do think might happen next, and why?" Open-ended questions often produce unexpected and revealing responses, and we should not let them be squeezed out by the rush to move on. Tackling such questions in a group is good too, as a contrast to the more convergent ways of thinking which a content-laden National Curriculum can generate.

Differences which affect learning

To make differentiation work we start by identifying the most important factors which may affect learning. One of the most obvious, beyond the first year of schooling, is reading ability, and there are many others which we can find from our common sense and experience. If you wish, take a moment here and jot down a list of the factors you think are important.

If our list of 'learning variables' is going to be useful to us, it'll have to be quite specific. 'Motivation' is one people always come up with, particularly in secondary schools, but that doesn't help us very much until we talk about the factors which help or hinder motivation. 'Intelligence' is another problematic one, leading us straight into what we mean by it. Is it one single factor, or a combination of 'intelligences'? This discussion, like the one about 'ability grouping' in schools, is usually pretty intense, and reveals fundamental attitudes we all hold about learning and children, about 'nature vs nurture', about the genetic or social influences on human development. No group of teachers will often agree about all this, but the discussion is very salutary, if we can manage it without fracturing our personal relationships. It's much more worthy of our attention, in my view, than the endless arguments about uniform and ear-rings, and which way up and down the stairs.

Out of this discussion, or your own personal reflection, may come a list of factors which looks a bit like this:

Some factors which can affect children's learning, which we need to be aware of and consider when we design learning tasks for our pupils:

- reading ability, confidence and speed

- writing ability, confidence and speed

- concentration span

- spatial awareness

- hand-eye co-ordination

- ability to listen to instructions and absorb information aurally

- ability to absorb information visually, from pictures or diagrams

- skill in manipulating numbers

- functioning of the child's senses, particularly sight and hearing

- learning style, i.e. the approach to learning which the learner feels most comfortable with, and his/her ability to learn in different ways when the circumstances change

- the child's previous experience, knowledge and skills already acquired

- support and encouragement from parents

- self-esteem

- high or low expectations, from themselves, their peers, their families and their teachers

- the belief among teachers and schools that they can make a difference

Your list will probably include some of the same ideas, but differently expressed. It may omit some of these and include others. It may be in a different order, although there's no priority order intended here. Before we get into the strategies which we could use to recognise and meet these needs, the issue is so emotive and fundamental that it's worth pursuing a little further. This may look like a diversion off the main track of our thinking here, but it's not, so stay with me.

The people most familiar with these factors will be those of us with training in Special Needs, who spend their professional lives identifying and meeting the particular needs of 'special' children, either in mainstream or in special schools. But when you think about it, there's no absolute distinction between 'special' and 'ordinary' children. What we are talking about here is the **recognition of individual need**, which affects all children, not just a few. I'm not presenting a case for or against 'mainstreaming' or 'special schools': wherever our pupils are educated, all of them, to varying degrees and in varying ways, have individual needs which we will try to accommodate when we teach them.

"Wait just a minute", says the hard-pressed teacher. "Are you saying that I am responsible for all this for every child I teach? What about John in my Year 7 geography class who cannot read? Is it my job to teach him to read, or to teach him geography?" No wonder we get angry about this sometimes: it looks as if we are being set up to fail, again. What probably happens in reality is this. John is already 12 and still struggling with his reading. He's getting extra help from a specialist within the school and slowly improving, but his skills and confidence are still below the level assumed in the work he gets in most of his classes. His geography teacher can help both him and other children in the year group by checking the actual reading age of the written materials they are using, or asking the Special Needs person to do this for her. (In some schools they have a software program which can check reading age of written resources very quickly.) If there is a gap between the reading age of the materials and that of some of the children, the reading specialist will suggest ways in which the language and structures could be simplified without losing the concepts involved. Just putting fewer words on the page will help children whose reading confidence is undermined by solid pages of print. The geography teacher is not teaching John to read but working with someone who is. If John still can't cope with the printed word, the instructions for the task

29

could be put on tape, so that John can hear what the words say as well as see them in front of him.

It takes time, energy and money too to create these added opportunities for John to learn in geography, but that's what differentiation is about. The pay–off for the teacher and the school may be that John is less likely to behave badly in geography if he is involved in the work and not constantly confronted with evidence of his own 'inadequacy'. If we analysed all the instances of disruptive behaviour in classrooms, some of them (not all) would undoubtedly be resolved if the learning we offered to pupils was better suited to their needs.

This connection between inappropriate tasks and disruptive behaviour, disaffection or even truancy applies also to pupils for whom the work is not challenging enough. They may finish given tasks ahead of their classmates and get bored waiting for them to catch up. They may be asked to do 'more of the same' and distract others for company. They may never have the chance at school to pursue their special interest, in which they might be more expert than their teacher. They may at some stage decide they could learn more by staying away from school or from some lessons rather than turning up. They may never have to struggle or experience failure in the early years of schooling, and then give up too easily when the going gets harder. They may get used to being 'top dog' and not cope well in a different climate – in first year Higher Education, for example. Sometimes the frustrations of these pupils are less easy to spot because they have developed ways of masking or dealing with their feelings which do not attract attention or get them into trouble, but even so these pupils have as much right as anyone else to have their individual needs both recognised and met.

Some achievable strategies for improving differentiation

For many teachers in many schools, absolute differentiation – that is the perfect match, at all times, between learning needs and teaching provision – is unattainable, unless we reduce the numbers of children in classes, give teachers more time to plan for and focus on individual children, and increase the amount we can spend on materials and resources. As none of these are likely to occur in the foreseeable future, we need to set ourselves achievable targets and be content with as many steps down the road towards better differentiation as we can manage.

'Content' may be the wrong word: it implies that the compromise involved is OK, when really it's not, and the struggle for a better education for all our children is a constant one. But if we wind ourselves up too much about the inadequacy of what we can achieve we may waste energy which could be used elsewhere.

Finding out about children's learning needs

1. Make sure that information about learning from the previous teacher or school actually reaches the child's next teacher. The previous teacher, having taught the child probably for a year, will know far more about them than we can find out in a few days or weeks, by which time we could have reached some wrong or inadequate conclusions. There's more about this in the next chapter.

2. When seeking information from the previous teacher or school, our questions about individuals' specific learning needs should go beyond the 'special needs' check, which often works pretty well, to include each child.

3. Teachers receiving children need persuading, encouraging and supporting to actually read and consider the implications of the information about them which is available. 'Fresh start' may work for new relationships and behaviour, but in learning terms we cannot afford to ignore what previous colleagues have identified and start all over again.

   > *A primary school decided to focus on this issue. First the teachers decided what it was that the providing teacher was happy to send on and which the receiving teacher would find useful. Then each receiving teacher was given half a day's supply cover within the first two weeks of the new school year to go carefully through the records and examples of the children's work, to observe the children if she wished while someone else managed the class, and to check what she read and noticed against her own plans for each child and the group as a whole. Another school had adopted the same process but the Headteacher took each class for half a day, to relieve the teacher and to give her (the Head) the chance to reacquaint herself with all the children, and them with her, and to have a good look at the new children she had not met before.*

4. The activities we design for children in the first few weeks of our acquaintance with them are designed to generate specific information about the skills and concepts which underpin what we plan to offer them. During this time we observe children as closely as we can, avoiding personal assumptions – our knowledge of other siblings for example – and using the clues about learning offered by the previous teacher as our starting point.

5. Ask for and look at the curriculum plans from the previous year which will give a broad indication of the kinds of

experiences children have been offered, and **how** they have worked as well as what they may have learned.

6. As a general rule, when starting a new piece of work or topic, ask the children to tell you what they already know about it. This is doubly useful, first as a check that they are not merely repeating something, and second as a way of showing how much has been learned by the end of the topic, which can be motivating for the children, and for the teacher too. If children say to you, as they often do, "We've done this before", check a little further and connect what they may already know with what you're now going to offer them. It might slow down your teaching a little, but it could speed up their learning.

> *For all sorts of reasons, a secondary school agreed a common format for the presentation of schemes of work. Rather than insist that everyone immediately re-write all their existing schemes into the new format, the Principal asked that this be done just for the first term of the first year, and that these schemes would then be 'blown up' to bigger size and displayed together on the staff room wall. Very quickly it became clear where the overlaps were across the pupils' learning in different parts of the school and teachers were better able to make these connections with their pupils rather than leaving it to the pupils to do so unaided if they could. The teachers also realised that if they could manage some of these overlaps more efficiently it could save time, not much but enough to make the effort worthwhile. They invested some time to save time.*

7. When planning, teaching, 'marking', recording the outcomes of assessment and feeding it back to the pupils, be quite specific in what you're looking for. Tell the pupils, and then give them specific feedback. Encourage them to

decide a particular aspect of their work that they're going to improve next time: this may well be a different target for each child, and address how they work as well as what they want to achieve as an outcome. Someone needs to write this target down or else it will be forgotten, and not referred back to. Training the children to be responsible for noting down and referring back to their personal learning targets is really helpful, for them and their teacher in the short term, and for the pupil as a life-long learning habit.

8. Among your record–keeping systems, try to find room for a place to note the particular specific things which you notice from time to time about the pupils' learning. Primary teachers often do this as a matter of course: secondary teachers see more children less frequently which makes it more difficult. An exercise book for each group you teach with a child's name at the top of each page is all you need. Then whenever you get the chance, using whatever shorthand you need and a date, you make a note of anything interesting as soon as you can after you've noticed it. If particular children's pages remain blank month after month even though they've been present in class, this probably means you've not noticed them, and it might be worth spending a few minutes' observation and thought on those children.

Strategies for making learning activities more appropriate for the children they're presented to, using what we find out about them

1. Check the reading age of any written material you offer children to ensure that it's within their reading capability. If necessary, put fewer words on the page and use simpler sentence structures. Read key items with the class or with particular children if this helps them to get into the task and keep going.

2. Make a list of all the 'key words', technical terms or common class instructions, which the children need to know and make sure that they learn them. Put them on the wall, or in the backs of their books or folders, and offer simple explanations and exemplars while still expecting that they will learn to use the correct terms.

3. On worksheets, give lines for less confident writers to write on, and space for those whose writing may still be big and less well formed. Use other methods of task completion other than lots of writing, so that pupils can show what they know without getting too bogged down with what can be a slow process. If they need to learn to write more quickly, give them practice and speed targets, although this will be an issue for the whole school not just individual teachers.

> *A colleague of mine who is an educational psychologist checked the writing speed and style of the whole of a Year 9 group in a comprehensive school. She discovered, among other things, that many of them had entered the secondary school able to do joined–up writing, but they had reverted to printing quite early on, and now printed all the time. The result was legible but quite slow, and they were about to start an examination course which in some subjects demanded a lot of writing produced ultimately under timed conditions. The school had to reconsider its whole approach to writing, to encourage pupils to sustain their cursive writing and practise to improve its speed and efficiency, and to make sure that the sheer mechanics of writing did not become a barrier to pupils being able to show what they know.*

4. As a general rule, give more 'structure' in tasks for slower or less confident pupils, and vice versa. The pupils might all be asked to respond to a discussion or a video they have

seen, but some do so by answering specific questions, others are given headings to prompt their writing, and others again are asked to provide their own structure given one title or starting point.

5. Use three-dimensional objects as well as two-dimensional shapes on a page, and pictures and diagrams as well as words to convey meaning, to appeal to pupils whose minds work better with tangible things or visual images.

6. Check that pupils understand what you have explained to them or given them to read. Sometimes a child can be completely stumped by a particular word and can't get anywhere with the task until the misunderstanding is cleared up.

The children were each given a cube and asked to find out its volume. Most of them set to with rulers to check its dimensions. One little boy left the cube on the table in front of him and bent down with his ear close to it. Then he picked it up and shook it and held it close to his ear again. Eventually he raised his hand. "I can't check its volume because it isn't making a noise," he announced.

7. If you have clear learning objectives for a topic or activity, tell the pupils what they are, and refer to them occasionally as you go along. It may seem blindingly obvious to you but perhaps less so to the pupils.

As part of a secondary school's focus on differentiation and monitoring learning, the Curriculum Deputy asked for some volunteers to undertake an experiment. For three weeks, the teacher would make a note lesson by lesson with a particular group what he thought he'd taught them. The pupils would also make a note, lesson by lesson, of what they thought they had learned. At the end of the three weeks, teacher and pupils compared notes. The outcomes were interesting, and one of the teachers involved decided to review some of his teaching behaviours in the light of what he found out.

8. If you can't manage individualised tasks for your pupils, decide beforehand what you want **all** of them to achieve within a particular topic, and make sure that this 'lowest common denominator' is presented in such a way (language, structure, time allowed for completion) that each child has a chance to achieve it. Then plan on from there to what you would want **most** of the group to achieve, presented again in such a way that the maximum number can grasp it or find it interesting. This might include offering alternative ways of going about the task or parts of it, and allowing

pupils to choose which they prefer. This choice might be about how a task is to be tackled. Some pupils work more successfully on their own or with one other rather than in a larger group. You may want the pupils to learn how to work in a larger group, but that doesn't mean they have to do so all the time. On another occasion, recognising different starting points, you might include some background information for those pupils who haven't met some of the ideas before, and let others choose to skip over that bit and start further on.

9. The third stage in your planning is about **extension** activities to stretch those pupils who complete the main tasks quickly and successfully and need to be encouraged to go further. If the 'ceiling' of the activity is set too low, and you have nothing more for them to do, they may end up doing more of the same, or helping you to help others. Teaching someone else can be high–order learning, but not all the time. If that's the only thing on offer when you finish the task, you might slow down deliberately to avoid it. What the teacher needs at his disposal in these circumstances is at least one activity, and possibly more to allow for some choice, which may be related to the main task but takes it further. It might be about applying what has just been discovered in or to a different context. It might be focused on the same ideas as in the main task, but from a completely different perspective. It might require further research and investigation to respond to a given question, or just for the sake of discovering more. It would probably require more and different materials and resources.

10. Provision of all the activities, ideas, materials and resources we may need to match the pupils' various learning needs demands a great deal of an individual teacher working alone. We need to pool our ideas, share them, use each other's, take advantage of the different approaches and interests of our colleagues: together we can produce a

wider range that any one of us could produce alone. In some schools and teams this works really well. If you need something to extend learning in a particular topic you just ask around and colleagues will offer ideas and even materials and resources. Better still, everyone's ideas and some of the necessary materials will be in a box labelled 'Ideas for extension work on volcanoes' (or whatever) which you can sift through to find something to fit a known need. In other schools, the culture is individualistic and suspicious. Requests for help or ideas will fall on deaf ears; there are lots of things around but no-one shares. We all know schools like that, and have ideas about why they are so and what could make them different. A sharing school is not only a good place to be: it can also produce a considerable improvement in the range and quality of learning activities for the pupils.

11. Sometimes, however engaging you try to make the extension task, there are some pupils who will avoid it, because they don't want to stand out within the class, or may worry about being labelled as a 'creep' or a 'swot' or whatever negative epithet is current at that time in that region. This peer culture is often much stronger than the adult culture in the school, and is one of the hardest areas to tackle if each pupil is to be helped to achieve what he or she is capable of. One possibility, to avoid the quicker pupil feeling too 'obvious', is to plan in extension activities as the topic or module goes along rather than leaving them all to the end. At various stages throughout the topic would be "What might happen if…?" questions, or suggestions for further research or reading, or an alternative approach which encounters more and different problems. The quicker or higher attaining pupils might disappear down these extended loops from time to time, but still end up in line with the rest of the group.

12.If you feel that the unwillingness of some pupils to excel is to do with the culture of the school, or the culture of the peer group, you may need to think hard and talk to your Governors and parents about it before deciding what to do. You may want to talk also to other schools in your community to see whether it is the same for them, and whether a concerted effort might be more effective. Certainly the research in the USA where some of these negative cultures are particularly strong seems to indicate that the school on its own may struggle to effect change. "It takes a whole village to raise a child " says the African proverb: the impact of the community and its expectations and aspirations is critical everywhere.

13.In some schools there is a very competitive culture: kudos is gained for being the best, not for competing against yourself, which is more private and personal and not always accompanied by public accolades and rewards. Re-emphasising that achievement is a personal thing, like running a marathon against your own previous time rather than being the first past the post, is within the school's capacity to achieve, even if it takes a while and may have to be spelled out to parents as well as children. Even the award of grades and marks could be reviewed to check whether personal improvement is properly recognised. This would be part of maintaining the self-esteem of those pupils who may not aspire to the 'norms' for their age group. It could also challenge those pupils who are content to 'coast' because relative to their peers they are doing OK.

Planning or 'Intervention'

You will have realised by now that differentiation is not new: it's something we know about, through our own good practice, experience and common sense. All these suggested strategies are taken from teachers who make them work, and you could add more of your own. The greatest barrier to making it all work is time. Time for what? It could be time for planning, or time in the classroom. So far, all the ideas mentioned need to be pre-planned, or they won't work. If you have ideas for extension activities but the materials you need are at home, or in the staff-room, then you can't get hold of them when the unanticipated need arises and the pupil ends up bored or doing more of the same. If the more structured simpler worksheet is not available for the child who needs it they either struggle on alone, or rely on friends, or make a fuss, or demand your time in the classroom to guide them through it, thus preventing you from doing the other sundry things you need to attend to with the rest of the group.

This is a prime example of the fact that **if we don't plan ahead for differentiation the only way to achieve it is by 'intervention',** that is by personally mediating between the activity and the needs of the individual child. Such intervention feels to some teachers like real teaching, out there with the children, hands on, interacting, busy. That's fine for a while **but** it's exhausting, so exhausting that you have no energy left to plan, and differentiation by intervention becomes not a choice but a necessity, unless you rely on your class control skills to keep children on task even when the task is actually inappropriate. Further, because you spend much of your time in the classroom responding and reacting to those pupils who most need your attention, usually at the lower or slower end of the attainment range, there will be a group of children who do not demand your attention and consequently don't get any. This is what we could call 'The Good, the Bad, and the Missing' syndrome in the classroom, and we all know about it. Even in the child-centred primary classroom we know much more about some children than others: in the secondary school with its multiplicity of groupings some individual children can slip through almost unnoticed. I say more about the implications of all this for record keeping in the Chapter Four on 'Marking'.

Identifying and catering for different learning styles

Differences in learning 'styles' was on my list of 'differences which affect learning' and it was probably on your list too if you made your own. Most of us recognise that not everyone learns the same way, but we don't often investigate more closely than that, nor think very much about the possible consequences of this for the way we learn ourselves and the way we prefer to teach. There are many theories and research findings on all of this, but to keep it simple let's take just one reasonably respectable analysis and follow it through. The learning theorist I'm choosing to focus on is Anton Gregorc, an American psychologist who did most of his research and writing around twenty years ago.

Gregorc's analysis

Gregorc examined and analysed the learning of people of all ages, and came to the conclusion that there are two sets of factors which critically affect our approach to learning. One of these is our **perception,** on a range from concrete to abstract. The other is **ordering,** ranging from the most sequential to the apparently random. These terms are probably self-explanatory, but let's exemplify them. The 'concrete' learner will like to handle three-dimensional objects in order to find out about them, while the abstract learner is comfortable dealing with things 'in the mind's eye'. The 'sequential' learner will like to follow a set pattern when being presented with ideas or working things out: the 'random' learner will take ideas, facts, lines of action in any order and mix them together to see how they work or where they lead. From these definitions, Gregorc then established four main learning styles:

- Abstract Random

- Concrete Random

- Abstract Sequential

- Concrete Sequential

In any group of learners he would expect to find a mix of these preferred learning styles, with Concrete Random learners being a slightly smaller proportion than the other three, which were almost equal. He made no judgement about any being better or worse: they were just different, and all of them could achieve effective learning if they were allowed to be used.

Because learners often have little control over the style of teaching presented to them, effective learners were found to be flexible. They might have a preferred learning style but they were willing and able to learn in a different way if the circumstances demanded it. By asking questions about our own learning, we can discover which is our preferred learning style. When we then consider what kinds of activities appeal to which style, we can work out the implications for teaching. If we accept Gregorc's thesis about the range of learning styles among any group of learners, we then reflect on the range of teaching styles we have used. The question is 'Did I teach to each today?' or 'Did I teach to each this week, or this year, or ever!'

Here are some of the points which are always raised when teachers identify their own learning styles:

- If our own learning–style preference is very marked, we will probably only feel comfortable teaching to that learning style. Even though intellectually we may believe that the class we are teaching contains the full range of learners, we may have real difficulty following through to actually offering activities which appeal to the full range.

- Certain subject specialisms seem to attract certain learning styles more than others. Some parts of

Mathematics, for example, are highly sequential, as is the learning of a foreign language. Learning and using one's own language, however, may be a more random process.

- Some secondary schools have established 'faculty structures' with larger teams of teachers usually in related subject areas working together. This is more likely to be an administrative convenience than a statement about the curriculum, but still decisions are needed about which specialists will work together.

- English and Modern Foreign Language teachers may end up in the same 'Language' faculty, but it can be an unhappy partnership as the different areas seem to attract quite different learning styles, who are then supposed to plan and work together. Geography and History teachers don't always see eye to eye as learners either, even though the overall framework of 'Humanities' is often applied to both.

- If teaching teams do sometimes clone themselves, the children who do not share the prevailing learning style may be disadvantaged because all the learning activities available to them, even if planned collaboratively and shared across the teaching team, may not suit their learning preference.

- The traditional academic culture in this country (the United Kingdom) and also the examinations system (although this is changing slowly) gives greater emphasis to Abstract Sequential learning styles. Many of us teachers, who have been relatively successful in the academic culture to be able to qualify as teachers, have learned to cope with Abstract Sequential teaching, even though our actual preference may be elsewhere. For many parents too, and even some pupils, this style seems like 'proper' learning. More 'hands on' activities are consequently a little suspect or even despised. 'Parity of esteem' is proclaimed as the way forward between 'academic' and 'practical' ways of learning, but such parity is yet to be proven in practice.

- We may improve a learner's access to successful learning by allowing him or her to work in the way which suits them, but in doing so we may not be helping learners to become more flexible in their approach, which is clearly one way to success.

- We may wrongly attribute a child's failure to learn to a failure of 'intelligence': it could in fact be a failure in the style of teaching, and the learner would learn successfully in a different learning environment. All of us can cite cases of people who apparently failed at school but were considerably more successful in learning away from or beyond school.

- The way we assess learning is also called into question by considerations of different learning styles. These different ways of learning may be connected with different ways of showing what we know. If in the Maths test the pupils are allowed to handle the shapes they are being asked about, rather than just see them on a page, the more 'concrete' learners may have a better chance to succeed. The essay is a classic sequential form, which certainly does not suit all those exam candidates who are asked to show what they know in this way. The assessment challenge concomitant to "Did you teach to each today (or this term, or this year, or ever)? " would be "Did you allow each learner the best opportunity to demonstrate learning during this test or assessment task, (or the last one, or the one before that)? "

- The very architecture of schools and the size and layout of classrooms may push us towards a fairly restricted diet of teaching styles. The relatively small boxy room crowded with furniture does not give the space for movement which the 'concrete random' learner in particular may need. 'Abstract' learning needs less space. Art rooms often look completely different than any other room in the secondary school, bigger, more 'organic clutter', as one school inspector aptly described what other teachers might have described as 'a mess'. Some students, who may not be naturally good at art, thrive in that environment nonetheless.

- Even the abundance of items on display in many primary school classrooms and corridors creates a very different learning environment than that in many secondary schools. Is this important in more than the aesthetic sense? Does the physical environment actually affect the specific learning of children, and which children in particular? Could we actually stimulate more learning in a wider range of children by creating more visually stimulating spaces in which to do so?

Differentiation and Progression

If we return for a moment to the original definition of differentiation, it clearly leads to a reinforcement of the idea of teaching and learning as a cyclical process, in which we observe what pupils learn from one teaching experience and build on these observations to plan and manage the next teaching experience. Much of the time this 'feedforward' is handled by the same teacher as the pupil moves through the school year. When one teacher hands on the pupil to the next teacher, this continuous cycle of learning should be sustained. Continuity should also be sustained when the pupil moves from one school to the next. The experience of the child moving from one teacher, or team of teachers, to the next is what I am calling 'progression'.

Key points

1. Differentiation is about trying to ensure that the right pupils get the right tasks.

2. We need to find out, think and talk about the factors which affect the way children learn, and the way they show what they know.

3. Through sound assessment we discover the pupil's learning needs: then we need access to a wide enough range of materials, resources and ideas to meet those needs as far as we can. When teachers share their materials, resources and ideas each of them has a wider repertoire to choose from.

4. A teacher's preferred learning style will probably affect her/his teaching style: with care we can become as aware of the pupils' needs as we are of our own teaching 'comfort'.

One big question:

Which is more important – to give each child the best chance to show what he knows, or to be fair to all children by treating them all the same?

Chapter Three:
Progression

Progression may be easier to define than differentiation, but it has implications for us as teachers which are similarly problematic. In fact, these two demands upon us are very closely related. Both progression and differentiation require us to understand the learning needs and experiences of the pupil to date, and to build on them. When different teachers are involved, we also have to communicate with each other about these needs and experiences, and trust that the information we receive is credible and useful. In formulaic terms:

Progression = Differentiation + Communication + Professional Respect

Let's take the two factors in this equation we haven't looked at much so far - communication and professional respect. It's hard to separate these two: knowing how someone else works is helpful to build respect, and we tend not to communicate clearly with those we know little about.

Progression within the school

In a single school, where people share the same environment, progression ought to be easy: all that teachers have to do is to communicate with each other and follow that through into properly differentiated teaching. But within schools, both primary and secondary, effective progression has not always happened. What are the barriers which seem to get in the way? I'll number these in case you want to use them to consider what happens in your own school.

1. The **culture of teacher, or team, autonomy** in the school. Whatever lip service is paid to the school as a collective, through joint acceptance of the school's aims for example, in practice some teachers or teams regard themselves as different and separate from the rest. In primary schools the closed classroom door can physically symbolise this separation. The secondary subject team can develop quite a strong group identity as they work in neighbouring rooms or spaces: this assists 'vertical' progression as the pupils move from one year to the next, but it can undermine 'horizontal' progression as the pupils move from one subject specialist teacher to the next constantly during the day. When the pupil says, "Please sir, we've done this before", it might have been in a previous year, or even in the previous lesson under a different subject heading. In either case the response could be, "Well this time you're doing it properly".

2. Another barrier could be that the teacher handing on the child offers what she thinks is useful information to the next teacher, but the receiving teacher actually wants something different. In this case, there's obviously **no agreement about the information to be gathered and shared.**

3. The **timing** of the handover of information: it may be too late to enable the receiving teacher to make use of it, because he has already planned what he is going to offer the children. Receiving teachers wanting to plan ahead may want information earlier than providing teachers feel is appropriate. The 'shelf life' of some of this information about learning can be quite short, and the providers may want to leave it as late as possible.

4. **Too much information** may be offered, with the significant items lost in a welter of the less significant. As the judgement of 'significance' for a child's learning is best made by someone who knows the child, the receiving teacher can't

find the bits of information they really need. The teacher may go back to the previous teacher to ask for help, but this may be too late, or she may miss vital things, or be resented by the previous teacher because it indicates that the next teacher has not even read the stuff which took hours to put together.

5. Teachers do communicate with each other, but they focus mostly on some of the children who present more problems. Unless the child has identified 'special' learning needs, very little is discussed about them. It's 'The Good, the Bad and the Missing' again, and the **individual learning needs of each child may not be highlighted.** The problem here is probably the time available for the discussion, which may be too short to do more than focus on a few.

6. The information from the providing teacher may be relevant, potentially useful, timely and manageable, but still **the receiving teacher does not take notice** of it. Occasionally there is talk of 'giving the children a fresh start' or 'I only look at the previous information if there's a problem'. It's hard to say here whether the barrier is attitudinal or organisational. Sometimes when talking this one through with teachers you find that the first barrier is organisational. You want to make some assumptions about the starting point of the incoming class because that makes your planning easier. If you then take careful notice of what the previous teacher knows about the children you may find that your preferred plan doesn't match their needs and you may have to change it, and the resources and activities which are part of it. One way out of the dilemma is to avoid the previous information, either by not reading it or by undermining its credibility.

7. The **'fresh start'** argument is an interesting one. It's tempting because it solves the progression problem at a stroke, but we need to unpick it a little. It is of course true that children

do need to cope with different learning environments as they develop. It is also true that for some children it is important to let them clean the slate of unproductive relationships or behaviour and start afresh. But that surely does not mean that the specifics of previous learning can be overlooked. Perhaps the first step is to ensure that the information being passed on is actually about the specifics of learning and not more global judgements about the child's character or worthiness which the next teacher feels might adversely affect her expectations of the child.

Twenty years ago, when my own child was moving from infant to junior school, I asked the junior Headteacher about the information which was transferred. The two schools, by the way, were at opposite ends of the same playground. He told me that a list came with the children, with all the names and stars next to some of them. What did the stars represent ? One star meant 'naughty', two stars meant 'very naughty', and three stars meant (you've guessed it) 'very, very naughty'. Whatever other information was offered, I can understand why the next teacher might decide that a 'fresh start' might be helpful to some of the children.

If these are the potential barriers to effective progression from one teacher to the next within a single school, we can anticipate that there may be even more when progression is from one school to the next. What are the extra factors we need to consider?

8. The two schools involved may know very little about each other. The deliberate and 'market forces led' fragmentation of traditional close ties between schools in a given community has sometimes resulted in less contact between 'neighbouring' schools than before. Further, the pursuit of than an attempt to improve professional communication

and respect for the good of the children whom we share. If the two schools do know little about each other, it is likely that communication between them will be adversely affected. Information may pass between the schools, but it will not be properly absorbed or acted upon because the context from which the information comes is not understood.

9. The particular schools involved may be unfamiliar to each other, but there is a further underpinning barrier which may also have a deleterious impact: from the earliest days of initial teacher training we may be separated off into 'primary' and 'secondary'. We may or may not observe children in different school environments as we train. At the end of this process we begin work in a particular phase of the education service and rarely move outside it. Some teachers move from secondary to primary, or the other way, and very valuable they are too, but not many do this. In a secondary school, ask the question, "When was the last time any of us spent more than a few hours in a working primary classroom ?" The answer for most of us would be "When we were 11 years old." In the primary school the same enquiry about familiarity with the working secondary classroom would produce the answer "Not since we ourselves were secondary school students". It should be no surprise that some of us do not understand as much as we need to about the child's next or previous learning environment. We can, and we do, attempt to overcome this barrier by talking to each other and passing information in various forms between us, but still there may a gap. The children, and their parents, may actually be more aware of this gap between us than we are ourselves.

10. The focus so far has been on primary to secondary progression, which is only one context, albeit a particularly problematic one. Let me mention one more barrier here before going on to look at other contexts. In the primary

school the child is normally taught for most of the time by one teacher. When gathering information about the child to pass on to the next school, the teacher may present it in one 'package' for each child. When the information enters the secondary school, different parts of the 'package' need to be seen and acted upon by different people. Information about contact addresses and so on are needed by the administrative system, personal information will go to the person pastorally responsible for the child – the tutor, form teacher or year head – and information about the child's learning experiences and needs will be required by the child's new teachers, of whom there could eight or more. If the 'package' cannot be easily divided important information about learning may stay with the person who first received it and go no further. It cannot be acted upon by the teacher because the teacher may never see it.

An adviser colleague of mine told of visiting a secondary school and asking to see the records about children sent by their primary schools. After some delay, while questions were asked about the whereabouts of the information, he was taken into a locked store room and shown a locked filing cabinet.

"Everything's in there," he was told, "if anyone wants to look at it." The reasons are not as important as the fact, in this particular school, that the children were received by their subject teachers as if their learning was just then beginning. This situation must be exceptional, and it was a few years ago, but I offer it just as an example of what can happen, with all the implications it raises for both the children and their teachers.

National Curriculum Levels and progression

In the United Kingdom, and now in many other education systems around the world, a national curriculum framework has recently been introduced, which includes a requirement for schools periodically to describe each child's learning by a numbered level representing certain prescribed criteria. These levels apply from the beginning of the child's schooling to a point in the upper years of secondary education, when they give way to other forms of 'grading' associated with the external examinations process. In the United Kingdom we have nine levels, although only Levels 1–8 will apply to the great majority of pupils. In New Zealand, at least currently, there are eight levels in the Curriculum framework.

The learning programmes laid down nationally apply to children at particular chronological stages: levels are only very loosely connected with age. They represent the 'norms' of attainment expected of children at certain ages, but children may actually attain these norms at widely differing ages. A child aged 11 might be at Level 5 in Maths, and at Level 3 in English. Another pupil at Level 3 in English might be 14 years old. If we look at levels in each of the components of a subject area ('attainment targets' in England and Wales; 'strands' in New Zealand) these disparities are even more marked. A child might be at Level 4 in Speaking and Listening, but only Level 2 in Reading or Writing, for example.

The feature of this process with most implications for progression is the common application of level criteria to both primary and secondary schools.

What are the implications here ?

- An individual level should represent the same attainment, whatever learning context it arises from.

- Level criteria are described in words. If the level number is to be used as part of the description of a child's learning, and shared occasionally with both parents and children, it is vital that the criteria are understood and applied consistently, not only by teachers within a single school, but by teachers in all schools, whatever age they cater for.

- To pursue this consistency, teachers will need to share their understanding of the criteria, and look together at their expectations for children's learning, and at the actual outcomes in relation to the criteria they are all using.

This business of 'standardising' (i.e. reaching agreement about standards to be used in the judgement of children's learning) is picked up in greater detail in a later chapter. Suffice to say here that 'vertical standardising', among teachers from different phases of the education service, has great potential for increasing teachers' interest in and knowledge of other learning environments, through focusing on children, what we give them to do, what and how they learn and what the outcomes of that learning actually look like. There is no agenda for teachers more important than that. If these discussions are purposeful and well-managed, they can generate greater professional awareness and respect, and lead in turn to better communication between us. We are still left with the challenge of differentiation, but at least we may have the information we need and can use.

Some practical steps to improve progression, from class to class and from school to school

(These are taken from real schools I work with: obviously you would neither need nor want to use all of them, and some you may already do. A long list is offered for you to pick and choose from, remembering that each school is unique, just like the children we teach. No priority order is intended.)

1. As you develop long–term plans for children's learning, share them with teachers who may teach the pupils before or after you. Within a school, doing your 'big picture' planning together will cover this.

2. Try to find some opportunity to visit each other's classrooms, not just to meet individual children, but to see how the previous or next classroom actually looks and is organised. This could be achieved by 'teacher swaps' with a neighbouring school, for a few hours to start with and then for longer if you can manage it.

3. As you develop 'school/subject portfolios' containing annotated exemplars of your shared judgements about children's work, share them with the previous or next school. When you've had the chance to see where the commonalities and differences of judgement may be between you, try to find an opportunity to discuss these. The logistics are tricky: the same primary teacher will probably be responsible for Maths, Science and English with her class, whereas these will be of interest to different subject teams in the secondary school. A small step in this direction, however, focusing for example on one subject area for a term, would be better than no discussion at all. For this kind of discussion, about outcomes and levels, the end of the working day is not the best time because of tiredness and the need for some people to travel to the other school. If you can arrange for some part of a Staff Development or Teacher Only day to be spent together it does help, but this will mean planning well ahead.

4. Among a family of schools in a particular community, the sharing of a Staff Development day can have more just symbolic significance. Well planned, perhaps using the mechanism of a Headteachers' or Staff Development Co-ordinators' Forum, such a day could be part of an agreed programme focusing on a particular shared priority –

differentiation, for example, or writing, or record-keeping. If the need is for more 'subject-specific' activities this too could be catered for in the structure of the day, although the composition of groups can get quite complicated. Obviously, the planning of such shared staff development activities needs care, to establish a mutually relevant focus, to ensure that there is equal value for all, even to manage the logistics of coffee and toilets.

5. If the pressures of 'competition' between schools can be sufficiently overcome, some regular forum involving Headteachers or subject co-ordinators from different schools can be very helpful, so long as it has a clear purpose and some structure for its development. Just by meeting together, the Headteachers can give a clear message about professional trust and communication. The barrier here, I'm sorry to say, can be the disparity in size between schools which makes some Headteachers feel that they are more important than others, and behave that way too.

6. With a combination of shared meetings and the occasional opportunity to get all the teachers together, some very valuable sharing of expertise and experience can happen. This is where we learn to respect and value each other as fellow professionals. Some of this expertise may be in the specialisms of secondary teachers, particularly those in which some primary colleagues may feel less confident – Music or Technology for instance. In other areas primary teachers are the experts – assessment by observation, classroom management, reading, display of children's work, to mention a few. Recognising the expertise of a colleague does not mean denigrating our own, but it can be interpreted as such when relations between teachers have been strained by poor communication over the years. Professional confidence and professional respect for others build on each other when allowed to do so.

7. We can share more than our expertise. We can also, if the logistical challenge can be overcome, share resources and facilities in a host of ways: sports fields, drama studio, art, music and technology suites, computer hardware and software, minibuses and drivers. Many secondary schools see the value of investing in their own future, and in a broader sense than just encouraging individual pupils to choose the school. Some secondary schools have developed a primary base, in which primary age children can be brought to work in the way they are used to, but with access to a wider range of resources than is normally available to them. This provides also an invaluable opportunity to get used to the bigger environment of the secondary school, the size and number of the pupils, how to find their way around, and all the other things which most concern children facing transition. Other schools offer Saturday activities, with proper payment for the teachers involved, which are open to all children in the community and have many positive spin-offs for all those involved. Anything is worth trying which helps pupils to settle into their new environment and to pick up quickly the threads of their learning.

8. Once children have settled into their new environment, whether this is a new classroom or a new school, their previous teacher can and should be kept in touch with their continuing learning and progress. Teachers might be encouraged to come and see the work they are now doing, and be hosted by the children themselves as recognition of the importance of previous learning. Copies of the next year's report could be made available, if requested. Children might re-visit their previous teacher or classroom. Any or all of these strategies emphasise the continuity of learning for both teachers and children.

9. Before the progression event children need to visit the next learning environment, and reassure themselves a little

about it. I don't believe that children in general fear change, but some do worry about the details and need to have some of those explained, and to be clear about the support structures available to them if they need them. These visits take time to organise and need a clear purpose and structure agreed by all those involved: feedback is needed to make sure that the agreed objectives are actually being met.

10. Many schools have great success in harnessing the expertise and skills of the children themselves to ease other children into new buildings and ways of working. Older children can visit previous classes or schools, or be attached to groups of incoming children for a few days to show them around and 'mind' them.

11. The Record of Achievement process can be exceptionally useful to encourage children to manage their own progression through their education. Continual involvement in reflecting on their own learning and next steps lends itself precisely to thinking ahead, being assertive about your own learning needs, having the confidence to cope well with change. Much of the evidence of learning which a child might gather as he or she moves through the primary school would go home, but some specially chosen items might accompany the child into the next phase of learning. These would be few enough to be manageable by the next teacher, and significant enough to be of interest. Two examples of the child's unaided writing, one taken from the beginning of the year and one from the end, placed side by side, can reveal a great deal to the child's next teacher about strengths, needs, and the pace of development. The same could be done for science or maths, focusing particularly on the processes of investigation and thought. Some examples of the child's recent best work can be very revealing too, and prevent the next teacher being simply unaware of what the pupil can do given a real effort.

12. Display in the new environment of some of the best work from the last one serves the double purpose of setting a standard to be aspired to, and recognising the quality of what has gone before. I have also seen excellent displays of children's current work taken into the next school, in order to give teachers a feel for the work and standards of some of the incoming cohort.

13. Many schools and teachers take a little time at the beginning of the new year to let children talk to each other and to their new teachers about their previous learning, what they are best at and worried about, their hopes for the new year, what they really want to focus on next. Sharing some examples of what they've done before would be used as the opportunity for such talk.

14. The most commonly used progression strategy I've deliberately left till last. Unless some of the things mentioned above have been attempted, the structure, length, contents and use of 'records' will continue to frustrate many teachers as it does now. We seem to have invested a great deal of time in the past years discussing and designing such records, for use from teacher to the next, or from one school to the next, but there remains the lurking suspicion that these records are still not always read or acted upon. I feel this will only happen reliably and systematically when we take some deliberate steps to understand each other better. Writing down things about children for someone else to read will always have a place in any progression strategy, but will not be sufficient on its own. In fact, if we put too much time and energy into writing about children for someone else and then discover the effort has been wasted, that in itself can make professional trust and communication more difficult in the future.

15. The statutory bottom line on information to be passed on is often pretty minimal and offers no real guidance about

what we should aim for. As a first step if things have not worked well so far in your school, why not try for fewer items of information but make sure they actually work. One primary school I know has opted for a few items of the child's work chosen and annotated by the teacher showing strength, needs and the highest standard attained, one or two items chosen and presented by the child, the end-of-year summary of National Curriculum level (for the next teacher, but not for the parental report except at the end of the Key Stage) plus one or two 'suggested specific next steps' for the first month or so of the next year while the next teacher finds out enough to plan next steps herself. In the first week or two of the new year they use the strategy I mentioned earlier: each teacher is given half a day (through internal cover by the Head or by external supply cover) to scrutinise these samples and records and decide how to act upon them.

16. Above all, whatever methods we use to find out about children and their learning, and to give them the best chance to settle into new circumstances, **the fundamental ingredient in this recipe for progression is the ability and willingness of the next teacher to make her plans and her teaching suit the specific learning needs of specific children – to differentiate.**

Key Points

1. **Progression = Differentiation + Communication + Professional Respect.**

2. **If it were easy we would have managed it more successfully by now.**

3. **Where shared specific standards are used, common across age ranges or Key Stages, a level is a level is a level, no matter which age or stage it arose from.**

4. Progression 'records' are probably the least useful of all the progression strategies, but seem to absorb the most teacher time and attention.

One big question:

Why are some teachers so dismissive of children's previous learning ?

Chapter Four:
'Marking' or on-going assessment and record-keeping

If your early training on assessment was as rudimentary as mine, or if you tragically missed reading an excellent little book on assessment (written by myself, modest as ever, in 1991), your first experience of assessment may have been the first pile of children's work you were required to 'mark'. Teachers of very young children will use observation and listening as the main check on children's learning, but as soon as the outcomes of learning begin to appear on paper, 'marking' becomes part of teachers' and children's daily experience. For many secondary school teachers, 'marking' is the most time-consuming professional activity outside the classroom. I'm using inverted commas round the term because, familiar as it may be to us, the word has a specific meaning: it denotes the annotation, using symbols as well as words, which we add to written work as we read it. Sometimes we add nothing at all to the work except a grade or score of some kind at the end. The Americans call this exercise 'grading' referring to the grades awarded to the outcome. Whatever we call it, and whatever it involves, this daily assessment, feedback and record-keeping is central to our teaching and to children's learning, and definitely worthy of our attention.

Every day, in every classroom beyond the early years, children and young people write things down on paper. In times past they wrote on slates; in times future no doubt they will 'write' on disc. Research conducted in classrooms reveals the vast number of hours pupils spend writing during their lives in school. What happens to all this writing? Occasionally nothing at all happens to it: it is not even read. More often it is read, to discover what the pupil may have done with and learned from a given task, and 'marked'. The 'mark' might be a tick at the end, which indicates only that the work has been read. If a score or grade of some kind is added, some judgement has been made about the work, but the pupil may still be unsure about the nature of the judgement. The grade could denote some comparison between this work and the work of other pupils. Or it could indicate the degree of achievement of particular criteria or standards. Or it could indicate the progress the pupil has made relative to earlier work, or the effort they are judged to have made. In my experience, before the onset of the National Curriculum with its specific criteria, most marking, in secondary schools at least, reflected fairly crude comparative judgement.

Looking back on my years in the classroom, I'm not happy about the way I approached marking as a secondary teacher. I was clear that marking should give my pupils feedback about their work so that they could improve it next time, but I was overwhelmed by the sheer quantity of it, not always clear about what I was looking for, and often distracted by the cosmetics of presentation rather than the knowledge or understanding which took a little longer to spot. In my first year of teaching I had four exam classes, two of which were for Advanced Level History which seemed to involve an inordinate amount of essay writing. I also had several other classes of younger pupils, all of whose books had to be marked with reasonable frequency, but I got bogged down by it, and fell behind, so that work might be marked weeks after it was completed, when any feedback was no longer of interest to the children or of great relevance to their learning. Not infrequently, late in the evening, half–way through a pile of books or essays which never seemed to diminish, I asked myself what was the point of it all. I knew that I had to recognise that the work had been read, but specific feedback demanded more than that. Without more careful scrutiny of what they'd done, I had little to say to them when work was returned, they took less notice, and my dissatisfaction with the whole process grew. By the time the nightly routine of marking had been completed I was usually too tired to put enough energy into planning, or creative ideas, or the essential details which can so affect a teacher's day.

Little of this dissatisfaction could have been deduced from my 'mark-book', a large buff coloured commercially printed creation, containing hundreds of pink lines dividing large pages into thousands of little boxes, into which I carefully inserted the codes, grades and symbols derived from the rather cursory assessment process. At a glance everything appeared to be in order: there was something in every box, but what did it all mean? Not much actually. What impact did this relentless effort have on my teaching or the pupils' learning? Too hard to judge, and it never occurred to me to try. Of course, this was a long time ago, and in many schools many teachers have moved on to more meaningful and manageable ways of assessing and recording pupils' daily learning. Some have moved on, but some have not. Marking is such a familiar part of the teaching routine that it has stubbornly resisted change over decades and still constitutes an area of our professional lives much in need of review. We must ask, and keep asking, "Why are we doing this, and who is it for?"

Enough of these maudlin ramblings. Let's take a more structured and robust look at the issue, to see **how daily assessment and feedback might be made both more effective and efficient.**

1. Ask some serious questions about the amount and nature of the written work we require of pupils. Writing is important, of course, but it is also a convenient way of keeping numbers of potentially noisy children ostensibly on task. They look busy while they're doing it, but are they always actually learning anything? Might there be a different way to achieve the learning objectives we had in

mind, which would lead to different methods of assessment – by observation and listening for example? Perhaps it's the relative difficulty of managing such assessment methods which encourages us to require pupils to write everything down. Pupils too seem to equate writing with working and working with writing. After a stimulating activity, plenty of discussion, learning light bulbs going off all over the place, children often ask whether they're going to do any work today. Their parents also like to see the outcomes of classroom learning: what's written in the exercise books and files is reassuringly tangible. Thinking again about teaching method and the mode of presenting outcomes doesn't reduce the amount of assessment, but it could provide a wider range of information and reduce the chore of writing for the children and marking for the teacher.

2. Decide the **purpose** of your marking, and follow through. If the purpose is to check that children have completed the task, that's what you look for. If the purpose is to see that each child has improved on the last piece they did, what you look for may be particular to each child. If you and the class have agreed on the specific characteristics to be achieved in a piece, focus on those as you annotate, grade and feedback. A voice at the back of your head may whisper insistently that the real purpose of your marking is to show the parents that you're doing your job, or to keep at bay the Head of Department who demands to see your mark book every month. Marking for accountability is fine, but the first accountability is to the child who's done the work, and to their improved learning. To achieve the latter, feedback to the child and feedforward to the next learning task are what matters.

3. Make sure that your purpose leads on to clarity about expected outcomes, where appropriate, so that any codes you may use make sense in relation to these expectations. These outcomes will also help you to make more specific

comment about the work as you 'annotate' it. These clear objectives and anticipated outcomes should be part of your planning.

4. When you're clear about some, at least, of the expected outcomes, share them with your pupils in ways they can understand. If it might help them to be shown some examples of the set task successfully completed, do so occasionally. I say 'occasionally' because we have to beware of directing pupils' learning all the time towards expected outcomes. Sometimes we need to encourage them to respond in their own way, or more laterally and divergently. Depending on our teaching objectives and the nature of the task we make appropriate choices about the degree of guidance which would be productive.

5. Your ultimate aim is to offer pupils clear feedback which will help them to improve their standards. To achieve this you will need to **focus** for assessment and marking purposes on certain aspects rather than attempt to assess everything. The learning outcomes you have identified are your assessment opportunities: from them you select your assessment focuses (or is it 'foci'?) and criteria. The choice of focus will come from the curriculum 'big picture' I talked about earlier. When you're clear about the assessment focus share that too with your pupils. The feedback you offer them should relate to this focus, whether you use grades or other codes, or words both written and spoken.

6. Talk to each other in your teaching team, department, or across the school about the length of time which should elapse between the work being done and it being marked and returned to the pupils. This is a very thorny topic, but it's worth discussing if we can do so calmly and professionally. We all know that it is important to mark work if children are to be motivated to maintain their efforts. But there comes a point when the feedback is so removed

from the original task that it may no longer be of interest. Could you establish a guideline for yourselves which says, "Wherever possible, marked work should be returned within so many days." How many days? A week? Workload is a key issue here, especially for those learning areas which seem to generate a lot of written work. How can we offer feedback to improve learning without outfacing ourselves to the point of failure?

7. We know that the most effective marking is done alongside the child rather than at a distance. Occasionally we might be able to do this, and with a bit of thought we might be able to do so on a systematic basis, so that each child is given that close attention at some point during the term, or even the year, depending on the number of children you teach. There are other possibilities too for providing feedback almost immediately, and then using that feedback immediately to improve the quality of performance. **Consider this:**

- You devise a task for the group and talk to them beforehand about the expected outcomes and standards they should be aiming for. These criteria could be displayed so that the pupils are reminded of them as they work. When the task is completed, under your direction, the pupils 'mark' each others' work, using the agreed criteria on their own, in a pair or a three. Each pupil provides and receives three specific positive comments on their work and three specific points for the work to be improved. These points could be discussed, shared with you, clarified, allowed to sink in. Then the pupils are given an immediate opportunity to do the task, or part of the task, again, making use of the feedback they have just received. This second attempt could then be re-marked by the pupil, or by you, depending on your need to be aware of what they had each done, and to improve the 'reliability' of the mark, especially if this is to be part of a 'high stake' judgement about the pupil's performance.

- Implications? First of all, this process takes more time, even though the teacher may still mark the work only once. The time it takes will need to be planned for, and may reduce the time available for direct instruction. Putting that another way, **we may marginally reduce the quantity of teaching in the interests of the quality of learning.** Secondly, many pupils find it hard to begin with, and need quite explicit training. You might start them off with a class exercise looking at a given piece of work together, with you showing them how to look for the relevant characteristics. Assessing to given criteria is a learnable skill: with an early start, and plenty of guidance and structure to begin with, pupils' self and peer assessment skills develop. By the end of their school careers they should be practically autonomous, able to critique their own work and take responsibility for its improvement. Possible? Think about it. A third implication needs to be considered also, not just by an individual teacher but by the whole school. I mentioned earlier the reassurance many parents derive from the quantity of written work produced by their children and duly marked by the teacher. If we are thinking about changing the nature some of the 'work' we are expecting from our pupils, and consequently the way this work is assessed, we need to talk to our parents before change is made, to explain what we're doing and why, and how they can help in both supporting the child to complete the new tasks and taking an interest in the outcomes.

I can recall sitting in a classroom while on a visit to a school, talking to the child about the work he did and the feedback he received. "Who marked this piece of work?" I said. "I did," he replied. "And this

> *one?" "I marked Paul's and he marked mine." "Why does your teacher ask you to mark each others' work?" I asked eagerly, anticipating a statement about the benefits of pupil involvement and its impact on learning. "Because the teacher can't be bothered to mark it himself," replied the child. Presumably that's what the child had told his parent too.*

8. While we're looking at alternative ways of designing and assessing tasks for pupils, consider this. Instead of always setting and marking tasks done by pupils individually, occasionally offer tasks to be done as a collaborative exercise and also marked as a shared product, with the same 'grade' or other feedback applying to each member of the group. As with any genuinely collaborative group work, as opposed to individual tasks completed by pupils sitting together, the composition of the groups will have to be carefully considered, and some explicit guidance offered about how to organise the group to maximum effect. Through sharing their expertise, encouraging the weaker members, playing to individual strengths and keeping the group together important learning can take place, about all sorts of things as well as the immediate demands of the task. Some at least of the outcomes would be presented orally and visually rather than in writing to widen the range of ways in which individuals can make a contribution. These non-written outcomes would need to be 'marked' on the spot, by the teacher, or under direction by the other pupils, which would also need organising and take time, but would be more engaging for both you and the pupils, and no doubt generate some discussion about the specific demands of the task and the degree to which expectations had been met.

9. If you're interested in introducing group, peer or even self-assessment, you will need to think about the climate within the group and the pupils' skills in giving each other useful

feedback. These skills can be taught, developing ground rules for the class which the children themselves may help to determine based on their common sense and awareness of each other. Assessment and marking of the group effort would also need to be balanced by the continuation of a more individualised approach, to allow for the fair recognition of individual effort, but the variety would lighten the load for both you and for them, and can result in unexpected learning, more considered feedback, and no more work for the teacher than other methods of marking and feedback.

Keeping Records of 'Marking'

Marking is actually two linked processes – the assessment of work produced by the pupils, and then the recording of judgements made, usually in something called a mark book or a grade book. As I mentioned earlier, my mark book contained lots of very small boxes, too small to contain anything except symbols which represented my judgement of the work. Even the space at the top of each column was large enough only for the abbreviated title of the piece of work, the date, and something about the nature of the task – homework, test, whatever. The end result, row upon row, page after page, of symbols against each child's name, represented many hours of my life and provided me with something to say about the child when required to do so, although any specific detail still had to be derived from looking back at the child's work and dredging my memory to find something useful or meaningful. Did the size of the boxes in my mark book determine the information which went into it, or the other way round? Surely it would have made sense to have fewer, bigger boxes in which to record my judgements about the pupils' work. I already wrote more on the work itself as part of my marking than I had space for in my mark book, but I was appalled by

71

the prospect of having to write my deathless remarks twice, once for the pupil and once for me.

Faced with the dilemma of record-keeping, it's helpful to go all the way back to first principles, consider the **purpose and audience** of records, and how we can make them both **effective and efficient**. So, what are the purposes of record-keeping? You can work these out yourself if you want to, and I'll have a go at it too.

- To keep track of work done, judgements made and next steps to be taken.

- To improve the children's work by feedforward from one piece to the next.

- To provide me with information from which to prepare a periodic summary for the parent or the next teacher.

- To show that I had both set and scrutinised pupils' work, and was thereby fulfilling my professional responsibilities.

The audience is mostly myself, although I recall being asked to submit my mark book to my Head of Department from time to time, so that he could check that enough boxes were filled in. If I were starting out again, and knowing now what I have learned from hundreds of teachers over the past fifteen years, I would organise my record-keeping differently, and design my own to meet my need, using the technology available now which was not available when I began teaching. What would I do?

1. Decide from the start that I would record more specific information, if not from every piece of work then from a certain proportion. I would not try to mark and record every piece of work in terms of all the specific criteria which could be applied to it, contenting myself sometimes with

noting merely that work had been completed, and perhaps a symbol to denote my general impression of its quality. Where specific criteria were applied, and the specific outcomes recorded, there would need to be some note of the **context** of the work, and some reference to my plan.

2. Each medium chunk of work, – the topic, module, unit, whatever we call it – should have a clear **focus** for marking and record-keeping purposes, which could be decided only after I was clear about the information to be gathered about pupils' learning over a year or longer. This focus would have to be quite explicitly stated so that the records made sense in relation to it. The record therefore would have to have sufficient space for words describing briefly the focus being addressed.

3. If my marking and record-keeping were to achieve any improvement in either my teaching or the children's learning, **feedforward** in the form of next steps for me or the children would have to be included in the record, somewhere, somehow.

4. Records in which I planned to record the anticipated outcomes of learning, with specific criteria built in to the structure, didn't have anywhere for me to note the interesting and significant but unexpected things children were showing me, in their work or in the classroom. I knew then and I believe now that each of the children we encounter in our classes is unique and special, even if this specialness is hard to capture when you see two hundred or so children and young people every week. Memory alone would hold some of the special things you notice while working with children, but memory is fickle and fades, leaving you with the less interesting things to say about the child, or to act upon yourself. Was there, is there, any workable mechanism for downloading from memory to page some of the most interesting and telling details about learning and performance, even for a teacher with too many pupils?

5. With all this in mind, the criteria for the design of a record-keeping system are emerging. It should have:

   - one section which is structured to accommodate information in either codes or words about specific expected outcomes for each child;

   - another section which is less structured and allows the teacher to make the quickest possible note of significant specific observations about individual children.

The first of these will look more like the traditional mark or grade book, but with some additions, and more spaced out. Here's a format based on one I heard about in a junior school in London, where the staff had themselves reviewed their records, asking the same kinds of questions I've been rehearsing above.

This is a medium-term record, designed to achieve <u>Context</u>, <u>Focus</u> and <u>Feedforward</u>

Topic: Brief Description

Date:

Pupil's name	*Specific assessment focus - criteria and methods*			Next steps
	1.	2.	3.	
(up to 30 lines here)				

Evaluation: (Notes to guide the effective management of the topic next time around)

Context is picked up in the brief description of the task or topic and a cross-reference to the bigger plan; the **focus** of the assessment, marking and feedback is written into the space provided; and the **feedforward** is twofold, both next steps for some if not all of the pupils and a reminder about the management of the same topic next time around. The original size of this record, by the way, was A3 landscape (around 42cm x 30cm), or an A4 record–book double page. Not every assessment focus would necessarily by applied to every child, particularly if the assessment was by observation or listening. Other children would be assessed and recorded on the same focus at other times.

6. Recording 'next steps'. The record format described above has a special section in which the teacher can note down the next steps which need to be offered to particular children feeding from the learning they have just achieved, or addressing a gap in their learning. To be useful, these next steps need to be specific and short term, but they could take a teacher some time to write down, and even then they will only be really effective when they have been shared with the pupil and monitored to check their achievement. To achieve a double bonus of greater manageability and greater pupil involvement, why not use the back page of a pupil's work book or file for the recording of next steps or targets, so that both teacher and pupil can have easy and continual access to them? The steps could be decided by the teacher, or by the pupil who is skilled and experienced in target-setting, or by both of them. They could be written on the target sheet by the pupil or the teacher, but will probably mean more if the pupil has been closely involved. The most important thing is that both teacher and pupil make reference to them, monitor their achievement, update and add to them, and see them as a way of constantly improving standards. Many schools and teachers have developed action planning and target– setting in the classroom over the past few years, encouraged by all sorts of schemes and

initiatives especially in the 14–19 age range. We have learned a clear lesson from this experience: if targets are not specific and are not referred to they are probably not worth committing to paper, and too many targets are as unhelpful as none at all.

One more thing about 'next steps'. On a number of occasions teachers have been puzzled by the idea of making a note about specific next steps because, they say, the next chunk of learning is about something totally different and nothing can therefore 'feedforward' from last learning to next learning. It could be months or even years before the next step might be relevant, by which time it will have been long forgotten. It is usually in what I call 'content heavy' areas that this problem is raised, where a succession of facts or procedures have to be learned which apparently bear no relation to each other. Two reactions occur to me – and probably to you too. Firstly, beyond or beneath this succession of disconnected facts one can usually discern some more continuing learning threads, either specific to the subject or more generally relevant to learning – choosing the right tool for the task in Technology, or writing with an audience in mind, or meeting set deadlines or working successfully with others. Targets established in these areas are likely to be relevant to the next learning, even if factual content is different. Secondly, I worry about whether learning is going to be very effective if no connections are made at all between one chunk and the next. Learning the telephone directory is impossible for most of us because it requires mere memory without the aid of any clear framework on which to hang the details we dealing with. If teachers don't offer pupils any framework on which to hang the succession of facts and procedures, it must be harder for the pupils to grasp and remember what they have been taught.

7. To pick up the insights we all have about the children we teach, some of which are quite unexpected, we need something with less structure, to avoid any pre-determination of what we're looking for. An exercise book for each class, with a child's name at the top of each page, would suffice here, or a set of file cards, one for each child. The book or the file cards appeal to different people and circumstances, and we'll consider the implications of both of them.

The file cards work really well if you like system and daily routines: I've seen them more commonly used in primary schools than in secondary. You write a child's name at the top of each file card and leave the rest blank, putting them in a stack. For a day at a time you devote the spare seconds you may have during the day to observing, listening to, thinking about, talking to, checking the work of the child whose card is at the top of the stack today. From the wealth of detail this process generates in your head you select a small number of significant items which you then scribble, in any form or code you prefer onto the file card, together with the date. This writing should take no more than a few minutes. If it does, try to choose fewer things to record, but never save time by generalising as this will remove the usefulness of the information. If you find yourself writing 'A good day for John', or Sunita, or whomever you've been focussing on, cross it out and start again with something specific about why it was a good day – what did John actually do or say which lead you to this conclusion? When you've written something useful about the child, put the card to the back of the stack and devote the next day's spare seconds to the next child. If you don't have time to write immediately, don't give up: it'll be a few days before the detail fades from your memory. Above all, if the routine of this process is interrupted for any reason, don't immediately give up in a lather of self-recrimination and throw the cards away. When you're ready just start again.

Some of us have trouble with these kinds of self-imposed routines. In the days when I was trying to diet, I would set myself a calorie limit for the day and the week, which was regularly exceeded, making me feel worse not better. Missing a day with your child-based observation and record-keeping is like occasionally succumbing to sticky toffee pudding: forgive yourself and move on.

If the file card system is just too relentless for you, or you prefer the greater manageability of a book for each class, the basic principle remains but it works slightly differently. As and when you notice things about particular pupils in any of your classes, download as concisely as possible, using any form of personal shorthand you choose, onto the child's page in the relevant class record–book. You may even want another page for recording things about the class as a whole. Every few weeks, leaf through each class book to discover which children you have recorded nothing about. Then become a little more systematic, setting yourself a target to pay some attention to particular children and record what you notice.

Whichever method of child-based records you find manageable, the information which accumulates in this way is extremely valuable. It adds a great deal to the quality of the judgements we make about children, for their parents in reports or interviews, for the next teacher or school, or for our conversations with the children themselves about their work and progress. Even if what is recorded is only a fraction of what we have seen and heard, the step towards systematising our attention to our pupils is worth taking. I've talked before about the phenomenon of the 'The Good, the Bad, and the Missing' among our pupils. Even the most conscientious of us simply do not notice some children as regularly as others, and some children work quite hard to avoid our attention. Here again the number of children we may see in any one week can radically affect our chances of keeping track of them, or even remembering who they all are. Incidentally, our 'missing' children are often girls, who may be less inclined to draw themselves to our attention. They get help from each other rather than from us, carry on with their work quietly and without fuss, and we may understandably overlook them.

> *Working with a group of primary teachers over two days recently, we talked on the first day about 'The Good, the Bad and the Missing'. On the second day one of the teachers wanted to talk to me. She'd been concerned at my suggestion that there may be 'missing' children even in a well-ordered primary classroom, and wanted to check her own knowledge of each child in her class. Without looking at any of her papers and relying only on her memory she tried to write down the names of all the children in her class, of whom there were 32. She remembered 31 and then stuck. She tried again, and once more, each time with the same result. She could not remember the name of the 32nd child. Going back to her class lists she could see which child she had forgotten – the same child each time. Her first task when she returned to the class was to seek out that 'missing' child, talk to her, watch her, check her work, and fix her more clearly in her mind.*

Checklists, ticksheets, and other such highly structured records

When the National Curriculum was first introduced in England and Wales in 1989 it was accompanied by some confusion and more anxiety about the responsibilities of schools and teachers in keeping track, through very detailed records, of the fragmented assessment criteria known as Statements of Attainment' or SoA. There were hundreds of these, with each subject or learning area being divided first vertically into attainment targets or strands, and then horizontally into levels, with anything up to five or six statements to describe performance in each level in each target. Oh dear, oh dear. Common sense and a respect for one's sanity would encourage us to treat these sets of statements as clumps rather than individual items to be tracked for every child, but common sense and professional confidence had been pretty well eroded and many schools felt that they must design and try to use records structured to accommodate this plethora of assessment criteria. Hence the growth of the dreaded checklists, with statements of attainment listed down one axis and children's names on the other, and the use of symbols to represent various stages in the child's exposure to and grasp of each criterion.

After several years of struggle and more explicit guidance from the central assessment and school inspection agencies we realised that checklists had very limited value because they lacked the three features of effective records mentioned earlier in this chapter – **context, focus and feedforward.** Imagine my distress, gentle reader, when I arrived in New Zealand in 1994 to discover that teachers and schools were being sucked into the same vortex, under pressure from the same circumstances, and were busy trying to sell checklists to each other. I felt, and probably sounded, like Cassandra, with much the same impact. When the great saga of the global thrust towards national curriculums and assessment systems is written we may conclude that checklisting is just an inevitable benighted stage we have to go through before re-emerging into the light.

In England and Wales, 'the light' consisted of the removal altogether of Statements of Attainment, and the re-iteration that assessment and marking criteria should be derived as a forwards projection from learning objectives, not backwards from the descriptions of 'level', which would now be used only intermittently rather than continually. Ironically, although this was the way that teachers had usually decided how to assess pupils progress before the onset of the National Curriculum, the habit appeared to have atrophied, and some teachers were quite sad to see the now familiar checklists disappear. If you still feel unsure about how to plan for effective assessment and marking, go back to the Chapter One on Planning, and have another go at it.

Key Points

1. **Marking involves daily assessment, feedback to learners and record–keeping for ourselves. For many teachers it is extremely time-consuming and needs to be rigorously reviewed.**

2. **The use of codes and grades for feedback is of very limited help in improving learning unless all those involved know precisely what the grades mean.**

3. **When pupils are trained to be effective 'markers' of each other's and their own work, their involvement can be advantageous for both them and their teachers.**

4. **Record–keeping systems should be determined by the information they are designed to accommodate, not the other way round.**

5. **Effective marking–records need context, focus and feedforward.**

6. **Marking for expected outcomes in the product of pupils' learning must to be complemented by some systematic observation of pupils as individuals, in order to spot unexpected and significant learning.**

One big question:

What is the maximum time that should ever elapse between work being done and feedback being received by the learner?

Chapter Five:
Portfolios

'Defining one's terms' is a rather boring starting–point for an interesting phenomenon, but the word 'portfolio' has emerged so rapidly onto the educational stage that it helps to remember its origins. My dictionary says that a portfolio is 'a case for keeping loose sheets of paper, drawings etc.'. In schools in the United Kingdom and all across North America we can now find such gatherings of 'loose sheets of paper, drawings etc' being used at interviews with pupils, parents, employers and providers of higher education. Groups of teachers are developing 'portfolios' for themselves, and sharing them with other groups of teachers. What's going on?

A portfolio is not just any old file containing papers about pupils and their learning. We are talking here about papers designed to be **presented**, to illustrate or exemplify something or someone: almost all the portfolios being developed currently in our schools contain actual samples or representations of work produced by our pupils. It could be a poem, a graph, a drawing, an essay, a photograph or a computer print-out, and each item would have some form of explanation or annotation, to clarify when and how the item was produced and what is significant about it. All these items have been **selected**, for a purpose and an identified audience. They have captured our imagination because they draw upon and highlight the most visually stimulating and meaningful of all the outcomes of classroom activity – the work of the children themselves.

As ever, to make our schools and our efforts effective and efficient, we have to ask the important questions first. For portfolios as well as assessment, marking, and record-keeping the key questions are "Why are we doing this and who is it for?" Let's look first at the reasons why we, or others, might wish to select and keep some items of a student's work. Consider these for yourself if you want to before reading on. It's mostly common sense.

Purposes

1. We might wish to show the progress in learning being made over a period of time by an individual student. The teacher might be the best person to choose the most indicative sample, or the student, or both of them. Selecting items is a form of assessment or applied judgement, and the decision about who is the most appropriate person to judge will stem – as with every other good assessment decision – from consideration of the purpose of the assessment itself.

   For example, if we want to involve and motivate the student it would make sense to involve the student in the choice of which items of her work to keep. If, on the other hand, the teacher wants to share with another teacher her judgement of the pupil's current grasp of a particular idea, the teacher's choice would be more appropriate than the child's.

2. Samples of work can illuminate special features of learning which we may wish to highlight. They could show a particular strength in the student's work, or a particular difficulty which needs to be overcome. Presenting an example is often quicker and more meaningful than talking or writing about it, and a portfolio can be used as a substitute for or complementary to a report about the student's learning.

3. A gathering of recent or current examples of the pupil's work can serve to show precisely the pupil's current attainment and range of skills. It's a snapshot with a very short shelf-life, but informative all the same. No manageable

sample can ever represent the full extent of a student's learning: realistic pragmatism requires a choice to be made, and that choice is interesting in itself, both for the chooser and for the person to whom the choice is presented.

4. Many of the assessment systems currently in place require teachers to monitor students' work in relation to specific criteria, standards or expectations.

   These standards are expressed in words and need to be applied consistently by all those who use them if the assessment is to be fair and credible. Such consistency will be pursued by discussion among teachers, and the agreements they reach can also be exemplified through careful choice and annotation of pupils' work. In this case, not all the items need to be taken from the same student: the sample reflects the shared standard, not a judgement about any individual. The purpose in this case is both to promote and demonstrate the pursuit of 'standardisation' in a standards-based assessment process such as the National Curriculum in England and Wales.

5. Where teachers are required to make 'high-stake' judgements about individual pupil's standards or levels, which may affect the pupil's overall grade, or his access to future opportunities, they may use examples of work to support and underpin an individual judgement. These samples should not be expected to 'prove' anything. Educational assessment is concerned with the most accurate judgements we can make, but it is not a science, and is rarely predictive, because of the number of human variables involved. Sometimes we use the word 'evidence' to describe the use of work samples to underpin assessment, but the legal connotations of this word are unhelpful and misleading.

6. Schools often produce brochures to present themselves to parents and the community. A portfolio could also be used

to illustrate the range and quality of the curriculum through examples of what the pupils have achieved within the activities planned and provided by the school. Some of the schools I visit cover the walls of classrooms, corridors and reception areas with well-presented examples of pupils' work, photos of children at work and beyond, and murals and paintings produced by the pupils themselves. These items could be in a portfolio with an accompanying commentary: they represent a powerful picture of what the school is about.

7. In the same way, individual teachers might use a portfolio of items produced by the pupils they have taught to illuminate the teacher's task design, her professional standards and expectations, and her capacity to motivate and stimulate her pupils. Of course the pupils produced the items, and might have done the same if they had never been in school at all and had learned at home or elsewhere. But as a profession we must believe that teachers make a difference: the fact that it's very hard to measure that difference accurately does not mean that we should not take a pride in what our pupils achieve while they are with us.

Audiences

Purpose and audience are closely connected, and in the list of purposes a particular audience is often implied. By spelling out the possible range of audiences quite explicitly we can sometimes see more clearly how a set of items might be of interest to a number of different audiences, and by pursuing and using these items we would definitely be 'working smarter not harder'.

1. The audience might be the child him or herself, reflecting about his or her own progress, strengths and targets for improvement. Learners of all ages, abilities and styles can

benefit from this process. On a week to week basis they might think about what they are doing, how satisfied or otherwise they feel about what they've done, recognising specific targets achieved or hurdles overcome, and earmarking an item they might wish to keep. Every now and then, but not too often or it becomes a chore, possible items for selection are sifted and decisions made. Some items are discarded, or taken home, but others will now be kept, and properly annotated so that they make sense to others as well as to the learners themselves.

2. Parents and care–givers too are important audiences, crucially interested in the progress and development of their own children. We know that parental interest and support make a tremendous difference to children's education. We know too that parental expectations of the child are a key factor in the child's expectations of himself. Anything the school can do to influence positively the self-esteem of children will help them to aspire and to persevere. Focussing on the specific small steps in the improvement of learning, and a continuing dialogue about learning between teacher, child and parent can be assisted by looking at the work itself, not just what we say about it.

3. As well as using individual portfolios to engage the interest of parents in their own child's work, we can use standards-based portfolios also to share our understanding and expectations, and the levels and grades articulated in the national assessment or examinations system. So long as the items chosen are 'anonymised', public display of a standards-based portfolio can add freshness and reality to parents' understanding of a standard which might otherwise be hard to communicate. A further group of parents might be interested in the portfolio put together by the school to illustrate the range and quality of the curriculum. These would be prospective parents, making choices about the right school for their child.

4. As pupils move through the school, each new teacher needs to understand sufficient about their progress and current strengths and needs to provide properly for them. In addition to the information, both written and oral, which accompanies pupils as they move to the next teacher, a portfolio of purposely selected items for each pupil can be very helpful, so long as it is not too cumbersome and reaches the right person at the right time. Many of these considerations were picked up in Chapter Three on Progression.

5. A further related audience is the next school to which the pupil is moving, which will be interested in the continual learning of each pupil. Some schools will use a display of the work of incoming pupils as a way of recognising and welcoming them into the new environment. Such displays can also be a reminder to the staff of the standards already achieved which must now be built upon and not allowed to slip.

6. At the end of their school careers our students move on into further education, training or employment. Providers and 'gate-keepers' making decisions about access to courses and jobs can all be helped to make good decisions by having sight of some of the outcomes of the student's learning to date. If they are interviewing the student, the portfolio can provide useful opportunities to get the student talking, and add reality and colour to the interview. Employers interviewing young people who may not be very skilled yet in self-presentation have told me how looking together at items in the portfolio makes the interview feel more collaborative and productive and less 'adversarial'.

7. Teachers themselves can be interviewees as well as interviewers: the audience for the teacher's professional portfolio would most likely be school governors or trustees,

finding out about the impact on learning of those they may wish to employ. Here again, in the interview situation, real examples of the process and product of the teacher's professional activity add life and context to what can sometimes seem an artificial event.

8. In recent years the Accreditation of Prior Learning has been introduced to accommodate a wider range or access routes to education and training. A portfolio demonstrating the actual outcomes of someone's previous experiences and learning, both formal and informal, is often a central feature of the APL process. The audience in this case is the APL tutor.

9. Some of the purposes outlined above are mainly concerned with ongoing learning and development. Others are principally about accountability – to the student for the fairness of our judgements, or to the statutory requirements

of the education system itself, represented by those charged with 'quality assurance'. The school inspectors, employed in England and Wales by the Office for Standards in Education, are particularly interested in looking at the individual work and progress of a small representative sample of pupils. The School Curriculum and Assessment Agency are more interested in the standards-based portfolios produced by teachers to demonstrate their pursuit of consistency. Here we have two different audiences, using two different types of portfolio, for two different types of accountability.

Purpose and audience are the two most important considerations in the development of portfolios. The next round of questions are about logistics rather than principle and can be tackled quite logically. Having said that, however, my experience of portfolios in schools tells me that some of the most well-intentioned schemes have foundered on the rocks of poor organisation. Think through as much of the practical detail as you can before you start, pilot the ideas to let the logistical implications be revealed without undermining the whole process, and keep everything as simple as you can. Over-elaboration is a curse leaving us exhausted and resentful, and prone to throw the baby out with the bathwater.

The most effective way to explore some of these practical considerations is probably through a couple of hypothetical case studies, describing the real circumstances and decisions faced by the real teachers I work with. To keep things simple, I'll choose two scenarios. In the first, the school is developing student-centred portfolios to recognise individual learning and progress. In the second, the purpose is to pursue the consistency of standards, a theme to which we return in Chapter Six.

Student-centred portfolios

All the teachers at Fitzroy Middle (or Junior High or Intermediate) School agreed with the idea of having a portfolio for each student, but their early discussions about it were dogged by anxieties about where they would put all the folders, and whether the school budget could cope with thousands of photocopies, and whether any teacher would have time to look at all the items selected during the previous year, and… "Whose idea was this anyway?". The Deputy Principal who was looking after the implementation of the idea realised they had to tackle some of the sheer practicalities before the idea itself was undermined. Her aim was not to drive these questions and anxieties underground but to welcome them as a way of moving on, knowing that any classroom-based process could work successfully only if and when each teacher was clear and sure about both the principles and the practicalities.

Her first move was to ask the staff to clarify why and for whom a portfolio of samples of work could be useful and desirable. Quite quickly, as part of a staff meeting, they generated and prioritised a list of purposes, of which the first item was 'to encourage children by helping to recognise their own progress, learning strengths and next steps'. The first audience was the children themselves, although there was also some discussion of the possible use of such a portfolio for parents, and even the next teacher. The DP then drew up some first-draft thoughts about how it might work, to share with the staff and engage their brains and experience as well as her own. Between them they drew up some early guidelines.

- Ultimately they would aim for an attractive and durable folder for each child, but these would not be purchased yet, until they tried out some ideas and were clearer about what kind of folder would be most useful. The last thing they wanted was a pile of expensive folders lying around unused, or at least not for their original purpose. In the meantime, the children would each make and decorate a card folder for classroom use. It was a good move to delay discussion about the cosmetics of the folder until the basic system was up and running: first things first.

- Once in each half-term (twice in each semester) the students would be asked to choose one or two pieces of work which they felt were important to them. This meant that the students had to be thinking about their work and what it represented to them as they went along, perhaps making a note occasionally, or putting a marker in their book or work file of possible items to choose. If these were copiable, the children or their teacher could photocopy them. Otherwise, a photograph might be taken, if something was too big, or three-dimensional. The DP noted that they might need a new camera, and possibly a deal with a local developer or the high school to get good quality prints. What she really wanted was a camera for each class, but that might have to wait for a while.

- Every item to be kept, in whatever form, would have to be annotated, and she suggested an annotation sheet like the one overleaf, to be used across the school. The inclusion of 'Next steps' at the bottom of the form was suggested by the students themselves as they discussed one of the purposes of the exercise which was to 'feedforward' into improvement of their work. The students also thought it was a good idea for them to annotate the items they'd chosen, and for the teachers to annotate the items they chose. Both teachers and students would have to work out the best type of statements to make on the annotation sheet, to make sure that they were meaningful to someone else and at a later date.

Annotation of children's work samples

Name _____ Date _____

Subject _____

Context (Activity, degree of support)

Who chose this piece of work? _____

What does this piece show?

Why has it been selected?

Next steps:

- The issue of whether the items should be chosen by the students alone was debated long and hard by the staff. Some felt that this portfolio should be exclusively the preserve of the students: others wanted to be able to support those students who for a variety of reasons might have difficulty identifying work they could be proud of, or which would properly reflect specific progress. When the students were asked for their views, the majority of them asked for the teacher to have the right to choose items as well as themselves, at least for a start. One child volunteered the comment that she wasn't always sure what was good about her own work, beyond neatness which was important but not the only thing to look for, she thought. The DP made another note about the importance of discussing with the children the specific objectives in a given task, and the criteria for judging its quality. In the end the staff agreed that the children should choose their items, and the teacher would add to them one more, if necessary, to complement the child's choice. The annotation sheet would need to specify who had chosen the item.

- While they were talking, they considered whether these items would be of interest to other people, beyond the teacher and the students themselves. What about the next teacher? As the student moved up from one class or teacher to the next, would all the items go through with them? There were jokes about the large vans the students might need to carry all the stuff away as they left school. And would the next teacher have time or motivation to look at all the items from the previous year? The DP made a few more notes during this discussion about reviewing the school's policy on year-to-year progression. In the end they decided that towards the end of the school year the student and the teacher together would agree which two or three items to take through, and that everything else should go home, still properly annotated, for parents and care–givers to see. They recognised the importance of some continuity from one year to the next, but also that the shelf-life of these items was quite short. So the items being taken through would go home at the end of the first half–term, having served their purpose, unless the student particularly wanted to keep them.

- The picture about who would choose what, where to keep it and for how long was getting clearer now. It seemed a little more possible and less unwieldy, and there were fewer jokes about having to build a bigger school. What they had already done was to assert that the most important part of this process was the reflection about work, choice of significant items and specific annotation, not the quantity of items. Given the thought and care which would go into the process, would the parents benefit from its outcomes as well? Of course parents could have sight of children's work constantly during the year if they were interested, as books and projects moved between home and school, so the items themselves would not necessarily be new to parents. What would be new and different would be the children's more structured expression of the significance of the items they chose. Would it be possible to use the parents' meeting with their child's teacher as an opportunity for the child to take his or her parent through the chosen items, pointing out the specific areas of achievement, or difficulty, or what needs to be worked on in the future, or how much progress has been made? The teacher might need to help out from time to time, but basically the interview would centre on the conversation between the parent and the child. Another piece was added to the guidelines, about the need to explain this new process to the parents, and explain the roles which would need to be played by parent, child and teacher.

- It was now clear that the student's portfolio would not necessarily contain a fixed balance of different 'subjects' or learning areas, and some of the staff were not entirely happy about this. Surely parents had to see the full range, and so did the next teacher. To resolve the argument they had to go back and re-affirm that the first purpose of the exercise was to motivate, encourage and involve the students themselves. Other audiences were a bonus. And after all, the parents would still receive the full report to which they were entitled, covering all areas of the student's learning, so the discussion of some items would be extra and different information. And the portfolio for the next teacher was just one part of the progression strategy which would also involve teacher-to-teacher discussion, records of specific learning outcomes and sharing of plans. So they finally agreed that it was OK even if a child's portfolio did not equally reflect all learning areas , and that this would be an interesting point to discuss with both the child and the parent.

- During this same discussion they came across another issue which needed careful thought, about the use of National Curriculum Level in annotating work in pupils' individual portfolios. If we are obliged to make defensible judgements about level in our pupils' work, and if this work is exemplified in the chosen sample and its annotation, then why not combine these two functions? One teacher expressed her worry about this. "These portfolios are designed to show individual progress, " she said. "They're not about comparing one child with another, or categorising what they do with numbers based on norms for the age group, which is where levels come from. How can they motivate all children if the level annotation just reminds Tracey that her Maths level is lower than all her classmates and the same as her sister who is three years younger? If I was Tracey I wouldn't feel very motivated by that." "What if parents want to know what level the child is at?", asked someone. "If they want to know, we'll tell them of course, and explain while we're doing so what the child needs to do next, but that's something different. We've decided that the first purpose of these portfolios is to reflect the uniqueness of the child, and if we're not careful we'll lose that purpose in the pursuit of something else." "What if someone wants evidence of the level judgements we're making?" came another question. "OK, to meet that we have our plans, our records, and evidence of the steps we've taken to share our judgements and make them more reliable. We need a 'standards-based' portfolio for that purpose, which would be a lot easier to manage than trying to put evidence of judgements for every subject into every child's individual folder."

- These discussions had spread over a couple of staff meetings so far, with the DP making suggestions to start things off, keeping everyone on track, and summarising the decisions made as they went along, so that they kept up the momentum from one meeting to the next. At the third and last meeting, some more important decisions were made. Firstly, they agreed that not everyone need be involved for the first term, and that those who did give it a go would keep a few notes about things which didn't work out as expected, or other important things that happened, positive and negative. They chose a meeting at the beginning of the following term to report back and make decisions about the next stage. Secondly, someone offered to write a brief 'circular' for parents about what the school was trying to do, why, how this might improve children's learning, and what parents could do to help. The Principal would have to sign this letter, but it was well drafted by someone else, and included a copy of the guidelines developed for the children and the agreed annotation sheet.

- A full term had now elapsed since the discussions began. Of course the decisions could have been made more quickly, but by taking a little longer for thought and discussion and the airing of anxieties the final result was much more likely to work. There were still unfinished details and things no one was sure about, but nothing ever works out exactly as we envisage, and they certainly had enough to make a start. The guidelines they'd developed so far were circulated, parents and children formally informed about what was going to happen and those teachers who chose to be involved in the first stage took their first steps, noting down some ideas and reactions as they went along as part of the planned evaluation.

Student portfolios for older or younger learners

The example of development outlined in the preceding section is based on students in the middle years of their education. For much younger children, in their early years of schooling, strategies would be slightly different, although the principles don't change much. Young children can be and are encouraged to reflect on their own work, although the prompts are simpler. Reactions to questions such as "What did you like best about your work?" or "What would you do differently next time, and why?" might be expressed orally, with the teacher acting as amanuensis, writing down exactly what the child said. Or those universal non-verbal symbols – the 'smiley faces' – can be used to great effect as children learn to make judgements of their experiences. Offered the right encouragement and structures young children are capable of very perceptive judgement, and the habit is an invaluable one, to be learned as early as possible.

In the later years of schooling, and on into college, work and life, the skills of accurate self–judgement, about what we do not just who we are, are a crucial part of what education can provide. Using skills hopefully taught early and practised regularly, our students need less and less structure as they get older. By the time they leave full-time schooling they should no longer need continuing outside help. They select and analyse items from their own work which demonstrate both process and product, the successes and the areas for development. They learn too how to use their portfolio to present themselves to different audiences, offering certain items to a prospective employer, and other items to a college admissions tutor.

Standards-based portfolios

A few hundred words back I reported the exchange among the staff of our notional middle school about putting levels, or not, on items in the individual child-based portfolio. They decided not to do so, and I for one was heartily relieved by that decision. Pupil-based portfolios are about 'achievement', comparing the child with him or herself and looking for progress and a reflection of the uniqueness of the human being at their heart. Standards-based portfolios are quite different: they reflect 'attainment' relative to a given set of prescribed standards. These words 'achievement' and 'attainment' are just shorthand for two different ways of describing learning and development. It's a useful distinction.

As soon as we start assessing learning in relation to prescribed specific standards we need to be interested in standards-based portfolios, as part of a general thrust towards more consistent interpretation of standards which is essential for the assessment to be fair as well as accurate. To explore the ins and outs of developing such a portfolio, let's have a look at another notional school working out what to do. Here again the issues and arguments all come from real teachers and real schools. This time I'll use a secondary school, with teams of specialist teachers all coming to terms with the imposition of a required curriculum accompanied by a required judgement of students' levels at the age of 14. It's quite a big school, with six full-time science teachers, one part-timer, and one other person teaching Science as their second subject. They're reasonably confident that the curriculum they offer accommodates most of the external requirements, and that their assessment enables them to check whether learning objectives have been met, but they're not so sure that their judgements are consistent across the team. They are also anxious that teachers in the previous school may be making judgements about level on a different basis, which may affect the continuity of learning and expectations when the children from one school to the next.

The idea of a Science standards portfolio didn't spring fully formed out of their heads one day. The starting–point was a departmental meeting, several weeks before they had to make their first judgement about the levels of students in Year 9 (all about 14 years old.) The non-specialist was worried about these decisions and was looking for help. He took a pile of his students' work folders out of his bag and spread them out on the bench. "How am I supposed to know what level each of these is at in *Materials and their Properties* ? I'm not even sure what the level statements mean.' He got the Science National Curriculum folder down off the shelf, opened it at the appropriate page and read the statements for Levels4,5, and 6. Someone started explaining what the Level 4 statement meant, someone else contradicted her. Someone else reached for the exemplar material sent out by the government's assessment agency, containing examples of students' work with a commentary about what level the work represented and why. The bench was covered with documents, several people were scrabbling around among the papers and talking simultaneously, and the person who'd asked the original question was beginning to wish he hadn't bothered. Perhaps he could go back to his first plan involving a class list, a pin and a set of dice.

The Head of Department decided this was the moment to take charge. "OK," she said. "We can't sort everything out at once, so let's just focus on *Materials and their Properties* and Levels 4,5 and 6. We'd better have a look together first at what the level statements actually say, to make sure we all understand the words, and then we'll have a look at some of the Year 9 students' work together and see what we think. When we meet again in two weeks please can you each try to bring some work relating to that target and those levels, for us to look at?"

At the start of the next meeting, they looked at the level statements in the three levels most immediately relevant to them. They underlined the key words, words which needed further explanation, or which were clearly meant to denote progression from one level to the next, and talked around them for a while, using examples to find the boundaries between one level and the next. Someone wanted to use a student's work to illustrate what he was talking about. They couldn't all see the one folder, so they chose a couple of relevant pages and made a few copies so they could all see it, and they each found their own copy of the level statements. The bench was getting crowded, so they put some tables together to make a bigger flat surface to spread everything out on. The example they looked at seemed to show some of the characteristics of Level 4, but also some of Level 5. They found some highlighter pens and began to mark different sections of the piece, orange for Level 4 , green for Level 5. On another piece of paper someone kept track of the conclusions they were reaching.

It was a useful half hour, and they went straight on to look at another piece which presented some aspects of Level 6, highlighting and annotating as the discussion went on. It was tiring at the end of a teaching day, but they felt they'd achieved something. The Head of Department decided the most useful thing she could do was just keep the discussion on track, suggest a break in the middle when they got bogged down, and close the meeting with a summary of how much they'd achieved and a decision about what they should tackle next, and when.

At the end of the meeting they kept the two pieces of work they'd been looking at, with the highlights in different colours, and the notes they'd made about them and put them in a folder. They decided to keep it in the stockroom with the other exemplar material so that they could all refer to it if they needed to.

An important thing they realised was that they needed to know what task the student had been set, and how much help he'd had before they could decide what level the outcomes represented. It was all right when they could ask the teacher who had provided the task, but if he hadn't been there the outcomes alone would not have been enough. The first thing they made a note of therefore had to be something about the task itself and the support received. Instead of writing everything out each time on a blank sheet, they designed a simple pro-forma. The name of the student wasn't important to this discussion: in fact sometimes knowing the student distracted them from talking about the work itself and comparing it with the 'standard', so they left the name off the pro-forma.

That was the beginning of their Science standards-based folder. From then on they returned to it when they got the chance, adding more items representing different aspects of Science and different levels and level boundaries. It had its limitations as a way of establishing consistency of standards. The practical side of the curriculum was almost impossible to represent using outcomes on paper alone, and they needed other standardisation strategies to pick that up, but it was a start, and a useful one.

Useful in more ways than one. Later in the term, during one of the periodic meetings with Science Co-ordinators from the local primary schools, the Head of Department mentioned that they were gathering examples of student's work, discussing them to share their standards and keeping the annotated items in a folder. It didn't take long to realise that some of the levels they were dealing with overlapped with levels expected in the primary school. "Can we see your folder?" was the inevitable question. "Why not? The stuff exists already. The only extra work involved is taking some extra copies of it and sending them over for you to look at. Better still, why don't you do the same with some of your students' work and we'll look at yours. Then we'll be able to find some consistency not just within the high school, but between us and you and you with each other."

It wasn't long before another potential use of the Science portfolio presented itself. Year 9 parents were due to receive a report at the end of the year which included the pupil's level for some subject areas. When the Governors (trustees) were informed about this they asked the obvious questions about levels – "What do they mean? What happens if you fail a level? Should students get a higher level each year?" Clearly, many parents would ask the same questions, and the school needed to do something to clarify the whole business before the reports went out. Two strategies were obvious: as part of the regular school bulletin for parents the Assessment Co-ordinator wrote the clearest explanation she could manage, avoiding all the jargon, and urging parents to come to a meeting in school for further information about what was to happen in Year 9 this year. For the meeting, she asked the Science department to put the contents of their Science folder on a display board, labelled with the annotations they had kept, and with the level statements typed up big enough to be legible and placed round the edge of the display, so that parents could see what kind of attainment related to which level statement. One of the most useful outcomes of this display was to make clear that a level is a space through which the learner travels, not a precise point to be passed or failed. It was perfectly possible for a student to stay within the same level for more than a year, still making visible progress but not yet reaching the point where the next level statement was the best way to describe their overall attainment. Through a display of students' work, anonymised to protect the identity of individuals, levels were seen in their real context, and the numbers to be reported would make more sense.

The idea caught on in the primary schools too, with the impetus coming from the Science Co-ordinators, and much the same process being followed. When primary and secondary teachers did have an opportunity to get together they each brought examples from their own students which had not yet been scrutinised, and had some of the most useful discussion they had ever had, not just about levels, but the tasks they set for children, and their expectations – all the things that teachers deal with day after day and need to share with each other.

Keeping portfolios alive

Both portfolios for students and portfolios for teachers are representations of the outcomes of the curriculum, and the curriculum itself is constantly developing. To keep the link alive between real outcomes and the items we choose to keep we need to take items out as well as keep putting them in. Children will do this constantly, as their self image changes and develops and their learning achievements move on. Even the standards-based portfolio needs to be reviewed from time to time: better examples of standards will be found to replace the originals, annotation made sharper and more helpful. Part of the purpose of standards-based portfolios is accountability to the external agencies, and the precise components of the portfolio may have to conform to some externally-imposed requirements. The basic motivation remains, I hope, intrinsic, concerned with fairness to the students and a wish to communicate about standards to the people on the receiving end of our judgements. **Portfolios can be part of what schools want to do, not merely what they have to do.**

Key points

1. A 'portfolio' is just a place where we keep examples of a pupil's work.

2. The crucial questions in selecting what goes in a portfolio are 'Why and who for?'

3. Consider how to keep the minimum number of items which will serve the needs of the maximum number of purposes and audiences.

4. Developing subject/standards–based portfolios can generate really good discussion about learning, tasks and expectations, if it's well managed.

One big question:

Is an achievement portfolio for every child really worth the time and effort (and storage space) it takes to produce?

Chapter Six:
Standards and Standardising

'Standards and standardising': the language of assessment is littered with words which have acquired over the years a patina (or is it a crust?) of perjorative and political overtones. 'Standards' are literally the criteria by which one measures quality, but the term is often now used to denote the quality itself, usually declared to be declining. Both 'standard' and 'quality' have been recently abused as words. On their own they mean nothing: they achieve life and meaning only when we declare our aspirations.

'Standardisation' also has a simple definition: it is the process whereby the standards to be applied are shared by those who will use them, to ensure (or at least to pursue) consistency. For those teachers who prize their individualism this process is unwelcome: even for those who accept the rationale the prospect of the effort involved is unattractive. This chapter typifies my fascination with assessment over many years: beneath the unpromising title lies a rich seam of issues about feelings as well as facts, and the potential for some of our most powerful professional development.

The challenging implications start from the simple definition of a 'standard' as the criterion by which one defines quality.

1. The standard is normally written in words, which in turn have to be interpreted consistently by all those who use them. Standards highlight certain expected and therefore presumably valued outcomes. The first argument may occur about the outcomes which should carry such a cachet: is it because they are the most valuable, or merely the most visible?

2. These expected outcomes may take precedence over the unexpected or less visible ones. How do we encourage and manage the recognition of the unexpected? If we are asking busy teachers to both assess and record children's learning, will the structured records we develop allow any space for the recording of unanticipated learning? The argument about assessing the assessable at the expense of the important runs deep and powerful: its resolution requires pragmatism and compromise, which purists have never warmed to.

3. The exercise of identifying outcomes can lead to the fragmentation of our concept of quality, as we search for ways to describe the complex phenomenon of successful learning. Mechanistic outcomes, such as motorcycle maintenance, can be broken down into identifiable process and product criteria, but flair and creativity are harder to handle. We run the risk of squeezing the Zen out of the art of motorcycle maintenance. Atomisation replaces holism.

4. In many areas of learning and human endeavour the whole is more than the sum of the parts. An extra dimension is needed to describe how the parts are synthesised by the learner or performer. We struggle to invent words to cover this eventuality – intuition, creativity, musicality, elegance. Sometimes the vagueness of these words is deliberate: we want to preserve the mystery of that thing we respect too much to pin down. There is a long-standing human urge to avoid or abhor the reductive representation of the revered. Analysis can destroy, it is argued, as can over-zealous pursuit of definable or – even more dangerous – quantifiable standards.

5. If we are intent on developing standards we shall at some point have to agree on the sequencing of the acquisition of whatever learning we are trying to define. In what order, if any, does learning occur? At what point in the continuum

of demonstrated learning do we decide that the standard should be set? Some areas of learning seem to have agreed sequences, but others do not. We still seem unable to find a clear hierarchy in the learning of, say, one's own language. Some learners, moreover, seem to defy the 'normal' ordering of learning.

6. A further implication of publicly stated 'standards' is the challenge of accountability of assessor to assessee, particularly when the assessment involved is significant or 'high-stake'. The greater clarity of objectives available through defining and sharing standards is of great help to the learner, but it could simultaneously undermine the power of the assessor, if assessment is being used as a form of control.

Assessment as control

At its simplest the phenomenon is about 'Give them a test to keep them quiet'. A more complex ramification occurs where assessment is used a means of preserving the distance between teacher and learner, assessor and assessee. Here the standard may exist but it is kept hidden or esoteric, a deliberate mystique which has to be maintained. Teaching and learning may be symbiotic in these circumstances, but they cannot form a true partnership because power clearly rests with those in the know, the 'cognoscenti', and excludes the student. Further, if the mystique is removed by sharing the standard, the assessor's judgement of the standard might be challenged, not only by one's peers (more of this later) but by the very object of one's judgement – the learner. For some teachers this is perfectly acceptable, for others it is a worry, gnawing at the roots of their perception of teaching and learning.

> *Ten years ago, I heard a young American teacher talking about 'grading'. It was in a small group, with an experienced trainer. Grading was the issue and there was no place to hide. The trainer gently questioned and probed our reasons for doing what we do. Why grade? What's the purpose? "When I was in school," said the teacher, "my teachers graded me. I resented it. I resented the power it gave them over me. Now I am a teacher myself and I do to my students what was done to me. It makes me feel better. I'm getting my own back." One teacher, one story. Typical? Probably not, but it's a fragment of a larger picture about the affective aspect of assessment, about power in the classroom, and the crucial decisions teachers make about it. Some of us believe that power is a finite commodity, which if gained by one party must be lost by another. Others of us see that power can be shared and that both parties gain. Clarifying and sharing standards with*

learners can enhance the power of both them and their teachers.

What do you think?

If standards are to be shared between teachers and learners they must first be agreed among the teachers themselves. This pursuit of consistency, both of the meaning of the standard and how it is to be applied, we can call 'standardisation', and it too raises a host of issues, both cerebral and emotional.

Standardisation

When assessment was largely a matter of comparing one learner with another it was less important to be specific about precisely what had been achieved, and energy was invested in the creation of a pleasing bell-shaped curve of results. In the past ten years in education systems round the globe all that has changed: more interest is now taken in what is being both taught and learned. The requirements of what is to be taught are being generated beyond the education service as well as within it. Some of these requirements involve practical or problem-solving skills which are difficult to 'test': a further and related trend therefore has been the recognition that teachers are best-placed to make these judgements, in the classroom, workshop, lab, or gym. Standards-based assessment of the **process** of learning as well as the product has greatly increased the active involvement of teachers, and their first task is to agree both the definition and application of the standards.

However careful we may be in the use of words, meaning is rarely incontrovertible. If teachers themselves develop the standards they are more likely to use them effectively, but the idea of a National Curriculum brings with it national standards which teachers then have to apply whether or not they have been involved in their development. Exemplar material, illustrating the required standards, helps of course, but can never cover every item of a specific assessment schedule. At the end of the day, the assessors will need to talk to each other.

Talk to each other! It sounds so simple doesn't it, just a normal human activity.

Think again. First of all, think of the scale of the exercise involved. The prescribed curriculum, regional or national, is a specific body of skills, concepts and knowledge to be taught, usually covering a range of learning areas and all the years of compulsory schooling. It is prescribed because it is deemed to be important for the students, and for the state which provides the money for the education service and therefore expects to call the tune. Having such a prescription taught but not learned would be a waste of the public funds involved. Learning has therefore to be checked as well as teaching: the output will need to be monitored as well as the input. How do we check output? Through assessment. How much assessment, and of what kind? A balance has to be found between the quantity and cost of this system-wide assessment and its validity. If the process is to have any validity at all, much of the assessment will rest with the school and involve teachers – and lots of them. All these teachers will need to talk to each other to ensure some consistency in the application of the given standards. When? Where? For how long? At whose behest? Who pays? Who checks? The simple human activity doesn't look so simple any more.

Before we consider these implications, it might be as well to clarify a technicality. Strictly speaking, 'standardisation' refers to the steps we take to achieve consistency **before** an assessment judgement is made. 'Moderation' has a similar aim but takes place after the assessment, to compare the results in various ways and to scale them up or down before they are finalised and published. Moderation is widely used in high-stake public examinations, but National Curriculum structures are so all-pervasive that moderation has proved so far, in the United Kingdom at least, to be too time-consuming and expensive to be feasible. Standardisation becomes even more important and is pursued through a range of strategies and over a longer span of time.

Let's explore some of these implications one at a time. For a start, why should teachers be prepared to expend precious time and energy on standardisation? What's the rationale?

- First and foremost, it's about fairness to children. In the British culture of assessment, and in New Zealand too, fairness seems to be the prime consideration, even more than accuracy. There is much talk of 'level playing fields' and less apparent public concern about whether the game itself is worth playing.

- For the individual teacher, faced with a plethora of criteria and an inescapable requirement to make judgements, the need to talk about the criteria as well as apply them sometimes feels like adding insult to injury. If fairness to children is not a sufficient rationale for the effort involved, teachers may also benefit from the reassurance of sharing judgement-making with others. Especially when the judgement is open to public scrutiny, there is some comfort in being able to say "**We** believe this level has been achieved," rather than "**I** believe...".

- The student and the teacher can both benefit from the standardising process: so also can others who receive or use the results. These 'audiences' could be the next teacher, the next school, external agencies of various kinds, and even government itself wishing to use the quantified outcomes of the education service to draw conclusions about its effectiveness and efficiency.

- There is a further rationale for standardising, which has greater benefits for the educative process: as soon as teachers begin to talk about standards in relation to real students' work the conversation reaches layers of professional thinking which are fundamental to teachers' role and skills. At an early stage, for example, we need to check out the context from which the outcomes we are looking for have derived. The questions now are, "What did you ask your students to do which generated these outcomes? What prompts, resources, stimulus and questions did you use? How did you get your students to do this?" In my experience, leading and witnessing hundreds of standardisation meetings, few other circumstances are so productive of valuable teacher talk, and there are few things more important for teachers to talk about than the design of interesting and productive tasks for learners. Great stuff – and if standardisation is the starting point, that's a rationale in itself.

Structures and models

Structures and models ! Makes it all sound very formal and organised. Sometimes it is, but the range of standardisation strategies is very wide. Some of these are what we could call 'top-down', where standards are exemplified centrally, imposed as tightly as possible on those who apply them in the schools, and checked rigorously by one means or another. Other methods of standardising are clearly 'bottom-up', starting with small groups of teachers discussing and agreeing standards, then sending representatives to other groups, and so on up a pyramid of teachers' groupings to establish shared understanding and then take the agreed interpretations back down to the grass roots. 'Top-down' is faster and tighter, but takes a great deal of expensive checking to ensure consistency of interpretation at the point of assessment in the school. 'Bottom-up' is longer and slower and expensive in terms of teachers' time, travelling to meetings, talking to colleagues. The most effective standardising systems are a combination of both. In sparsely populated areas the logistics of getting teachers together are problematic, but the spin-off in professional development may be worth the investment. In some small school systems, there could be great advantage in bringing all the system's teachers together in one place for a few days once a year, to talk and work together. If such events were well-structured there could be tremendous benefits, including more efficient and effective standardisation.

Before looking more closely at the full range of standardisation activities, let me offer two vignettes, as different as they could be. The first is several years old, but still very fresh in my memory. This was an event in New Jersey dealing with the assessment of 'creative' written English. The students had been asked to write a few paragraphs on given topics, which were now to be assessed against a given grade schedule. In a vast hotel ballroom several hundred teachers were seated around tables, with about twenty in each group. Scripts were distributed for 'trial grading' and perused by everyone for a few minutes. A whistle was blown, scores allocated by each person and written on cards. Another whistle blew and the grades were displayed simultaneously by each assessor. By looking at the grades awarded by others compared with their own, the assessors were able to pick up the consensus of standard and adapt themselves to it. In each group the leader looked for 'rogue assessors', who seemed out of tune with the rest or insisted on a more personal and individual response to what they read. I was intrigued by the whole event: the scale, the military precision, the questionable validity of the exercise as a judgement of creative writing, the lack of real discussion, the pressure to conform epitomised in the expressions as people looked round the group and discovered that they were or were not in line with others' judgements. I was merely a visitor, unaware of what may have gone before, and my impressions may not be a fair reflection of the whole process – but they were powerful impressions all the same, raising big questions about the compromise between validity, reliability, manageability and professionalism.

The second image is drawn from the early days of the National Curriculum in England, as teachers of young children wrestled with a curriculum more tightly prescribed than anything they had encountered before, which they then had to assess using level standards. These teachers had received little if any technical training about standardisation: their common sense and experience suggested a certain line of action. Firstly, the two teachers of Year 1 (5–year–olds) decided to work together on the planning of an activity, discussing as they did so their interpretation of the prescribed objectives. Having planned the activity they conducted it each with her own class and brought some of the retainable outcomes back to share with the other. They compared the outcomes to the given level standards, made some notes about the joint decisions they made during this discussion, recognised the commonalities and differences in their interpretation and moved on.

These two images could hardly be more different: in one a mass of assessors directed by whistles, in the other two people talking quietly in a corner of the staff room, but the fundamental purpose of both was the pursuit of consistency.

Examples of the range of possible standardising activities

- Teachers plan topics together, using the prescribed curriculum framework as their shared 'touchstone'.

- Teachers agree to certain outcomes of a topic being shared among themselves and discussed in relation to the prescribed standards or 'level descriptions'.

- Teachers look together at the wording of the given standards. They identify and discuss those words or terms which may generate different interpretations. They might, for example, need to discuss the difference between 'knowledge' and 'understanding', and what one would expect to see as evidence of either.

- If there is a given hierarchy or sequence of standards representing different levels of performance, teachers develop shared 'word pictures' of learners at different levels, and explore in doing so the subtleties of distinction between one level and the next.

- Where the performance to be assessed is ephemeral – spoken words or practical activity – teachers swap classes or look together at students at work and then discuss what they have seen. Video could be used for this too, not to provide evidence of an individual student's performance but to allow teachers to consider and discuss the evidence and reach agreement about the judgement they would make.

- Exemplar material provided centrally to illustrate expected standards is shared and discussed.

- Teachers develop their own exemplar material, keeping items of students' work which they have discussed and annotated, to use as touchstones for their future decisions. In England and Wales these items are often gathered into folders called 'portfolios'. (You may have already read about these in Chapter Five above.)

- If the school has, say, a Maths portfolio this could be shared with another school or more widely across a group of schools. Ultimately, if a manageable structure can be found, a group of schools together could develop a Maths portfolio for the whole group.

- One person is given the job of visiting several schools, talking to teachers about their interpretation of the standard, looking at the outcomes of their decisions, sharing with them decisions made in other schools, gradually bringing schools in line with each other.

Evidence of school-based standardisation

In the previous chapter we examined the development of a 'portfolio' in which the school keeps annotated examples of children's work which illuminate agreed standards within the school. The process by which items are selected, discussed and annotated is more important for effective standardisation than the contents of the portfolio, although these can be used as reference points for decisions subsequently made about standards achieved by individual children. As we have seen earlier in this chapter, schools and teachers can do a host of other things which improve the consistency of judgement making. If you wish to have evidence of your efforts with this, consider keeping a 'standardising log'. Briefly and simply, you keep track of what you did, when, and who was involved. This information might be gleaned from the minutes of team meetings or records of staff development activities, but this 'log' pulls together the information into one plac I'menvisaging a little notebook, with three columns on each page, headed:

Date	Activity	Who involved

The information could be entered by the Assessment Co-ordinator, or whoever is responsible for the quality of assessment in the school, and would monitor the range and regularity of the pursuit of consistency, to reassure yourselves or others that you are taking the issue seriously. It would take only minutes to maintain such a log, but it could serve an important and useful purpose in the school.

Starting points for school-based standardisation

In addition to any top-down system-wide standardisation strategies, there is always a need to pursue school-based consistency as well, for reasons of useful staff development as well as technical reliability. Surveys of assessment practice conducted by Inspectors in England and Wales have regularly highlighted this need, and schools are concerned about the quality of their assessment for intrinsic reasons too. In working with schools and teachers on these matters I find it helpful to establish a number of ground rules from the start.

1. Accept from the beginning that absolute consistency in our interpretation of standards is probably unachieveable, but that we should do the best we can taking one step at a time.

2. Some discussion of the semantics, that is the actual meanings of words used in the standard, is helpful. However, after a certain point it can get very tedious, at which time we turn to actual examples of students' work to help us exemplify shared meaning.

3. The ephemeral outcomes of learning are as important as the more tangible and retainable outcomes. Our assessments of these outcomes need to be standardised, but without the easy availability of work on paper which we can all look at. When a task is new and somewhat daunting, focus on the easier bits first, and tackle the harder parts later: doing so does not mean that you regard ephemeral outcomes as less important, but that you recognise your own need to work along an incline of difficulty. One step at a time, and keep going.

4. Talking together is both inescapable as part of a standardising process and valuable in itself. At first the discussion can be quite tiring because of the need to be precise and to pursue consensus. After–school meetings do not provide the best circumstances, and time should be

sought earlier in the day, and for longer chunks of time so that agreements can be found and consolidated rather than postponed to the next meeting.

5. All those involved need to accept that the aim is to find a consensus, which means compromise and a voluntary reduction in one's autonomy in the interests of greater fairness to the students and greater reliability in the assessment process.

6. When we use a student's work to explore shared interpretations of standard we have to focus on the work and its characteristics, not on the student as an individual. We need to be aware that standards can be emotive issues, so we maintain a clear distinction between our professional and personal views.

> *An incident: we had just finished a meeting discussing the application of given standards in children's written work. I walked along the corridor behind two other people who had taken part and listened to their conversation. "Did you notice," said one, "that Mrs Bailey didn't seem to be very bothered about the correct use of punctuation?" "Well I'm not surprised," replied the other, "Have you seen her house?"*

Have you noticed how many of these starting points so far have been about how we feel not just what we do? Feelings are facts and are best recognised as such, not swept to one side as immaterial. Basic practical things matter a great deal too.

7. If you are going to look together at children's work, make sure you have sufficient legible copies of the items for everyone to see and read.

8. Have sufficient copies of the standards available too so that you are all sure of the precise wording you are working to.

9. With all these papers floating about, you need table space rather than the floor or people's knees.

10. When an agreement has been reached make sure it is recorded precisely enough to make sense to you later, and to others who may not have been involved in the discussion.

Standardisation in practice

In my book about 'School Self Review' I included two hypothetical case studies to exemplify the process. To explore more of the practical implications of standardising, I'm now going to return to one of my notional schools.

London Street Primary School is an urban, two–form entry, 5–11 age range Infant and Junior School. Infant and Junior sections have not always worked very closely together but the new Head is making progress towards this end, and she feels that the shared framework of the National Curriculum will help. The Local Education Authority has suggested that schools should develop 'portfolios' in English, Maths and Science to assist with standardising, and the Head and Deputy have to consider how best to set about this. The quickest way would be to delegate the task to the subject Co-ordinators, or to the Assessment Co-ordinator, Marion, a very able and experienced teacher who could no doubt handle the whole job on her own if she was given some time to do so. Certainly a folder of annotated examples of pupils' work related to National Curriculum standards could be produced, but for what purpose? There must be more potential gains for the school than just having a portfolio to show to someone who is checking up.

The Head and the Deputy decide to share their thinking at this early stage with the Co-ordinators, rather than present them with a fixed plan. They begin by highlighting all the reasons why and how developing school portfolios could be useful to them.

- Agreeing shared standards would help to draw Infant and Junior teachers together, if it was handled with that purpose in mind.

- It could help in coming to terms with some of the subject-specific elements of the National Curriculum framework within the integrated topics which are the current focus of the school's curriculum.

- It would be useful experience for the Co-ordinators themselves, although the least experienced of them, Priti, said that she would appreciate some advice on running a meeting before she started.

- If all the teachers could be involved, some of the prevailing anxiety about National Curriculum assessment might be alleviated, and some of the less experienced teachers might benefit from the experience of others. The Head recognised that there was a direct link between professional confidence and the **quality** – as opposed to the **quantity** – of school-based assessment. Where teachers were unsure of themselves and their judgements they tended to assess and record too much, too often and consequently not very well. If standardising led to greater confidence the quality of assessment would rise.

- Some of the Junior teachers had sometimes been rather dismissive of the Infant teachers, but it was likely that on this issue the Infant teachers would lead the way because they had been involved in National Curriculum implementation longer. The Head thought it could be very salutary for all concerned.

- The Assessment Co-ordinator was very relieved that the assessment responsibility was being more widely distributed, and was very willing to share the expertise she had accumulated about how to encourage greater consistency and team work among the staff.

- Looking beyond their own immediate needs, they all agreed that sharing standards would produce fairer decisions about pupils' learning to share with them and their parents. When exemplar portfolios were produced, they could very helpful in explaining about levels and standards to those parents who were interested and already asking questions about them.

- Last on their list, interestingly, was the use of the portfolio to show to the LEA as 'proof' of the pursuit of consistency in the school.

This list didn't take long, but it was important to establish what could be gained not only by the school and the pupils but also by the key individuals involved. The strategy they now thought through had to reflect these aspirations. They agreed the following stages.

1. Instead of trying to manage all three subjects simultaneously, which could be both daunting and confusing, it was decided to focus on one subject each term, starting with English in the next term.

2. Before that, using one of the scheduled staff meetings, the Head would take the whole staff through the "What's in it for us?" exercise, and give everyone the chance to explore not only the positive potential but also the parts they were not so happy about. The Head had already guessed that one of the Junior staff, Audrey, would be less than thrilled

at the prospect of exposing her children's work to the scrutiny of others, as she was always uncomfortable with working collaboratively, and seemed to regard any interest in what she did as personal criticism. Audrey deserved the opportunity, along with everyone else, to voice her anxieties, even if the script could have been written beforehand !

Also at this meeting, the English Co-ordinator, Jane, would explain her strategy and ask for help with the fine tuning. Starting with Jane meant that Priti could watch and listen and learn how Jane handled the group: in fact Jane was happy to talk this through with Priti, and the Head began thinking – to herself for the time being – about a mentoring scheme in the school.

3. All the co-ordinators thought it would be easier to focus on an agreed topic for standardising purposes, and to choose a topic which would generate some clearly 'visible' outcomes to give them a place to start. So the plan each term would be to:

    - focus on a topic, and work in small groups to plan the activities;

    - all agree to teach the topic within a given time, and retain some of the tangible outcomes to discuss with the group;

    - choose one ephemeral outcome, observe a small number of children with some care, make some record of these observations, and be prepared to discuss the assessment based on these notes of specific 'performance'. In English, the focus for this observation would be 'Speaking and Listening' and in Science and Maths it would be practical investigations and problem-solving respectively;

    - the discussion of outcomes would require at least three meetings each term. To get the process off to a good start, the Head agreed to ask the Governors to change a planned Staff Development day so that it fell at the point in the first term when discussion of outcomes was needed. They all thought (and quite right too) that they would probably achieve more in three hours in a morning than in three separate hours after school;

- by the end of each term an identifiable start would have been made with a subject portfolio, which could then be added to slowly but surely, widening the range of exemplars and highlighting the trickier decisions about level and level boundaries. It would be really good if these items, and the topic from which they sprang, could be shared by display with parents, but they reserved judgement on that until they saw what materialised. So far, so good, but a few questions still remained to be resolved.

First, should people work in year specific groups or mixed groups to plan the topic? The whole point of the exercise was to generate a shared approach, and each year team had only two people, but it would be hard for the teachers of the 4 year–olds to relate to learning activities for the top Juniors. A compromise was reached: the early discussion of objectives and the prescribed outcomes would involve everyone, led by the subject Co-ordinator, with the detailed planning done in groups of four, each covering two years, which meant that the top Infant (Year 2) teachers would work with their Junior colleagues (Year 3) and bridge the Infant/Junior divide which the Head had been particularly concerned about.

It was hoped that Years 4, 5 and 6 would work together, and they would invite someone from the local high school to work with them too. The group would be a little larger and the Deputy agreed to help manage it.

Second, there was the logistical problem of trying to cope with the agreed outcomes from all the children at once: they would be awash with paper. So they put in an extra stage to sort this out: between the end of the topic and the 'standardising meeting' the relevant subject Co-ordinator would gather up the outcomes and, with help from Marion, the Assessment Co-ordinator, choose a small number of items which would raise some interesting issues, take off the children's names, and make sufficient copies for everyone to see. Marion suggested that they deliberately start with relatively easy items first.

Third, what about the group structure? Because everyone was dealing with the same set of given standards the standardising meeting would include all the staff, not divided into year groups. The Head encouraged this as it would help towards another of her longer-term objectives, – to encourage greater continuity in the curriculum and more understanding of the whole curriculum among some of the teachers, including Audrey. Marion knew from some of her colleagues in other schools that it was sometimes helpful to start with 'neutral' work, to pre-empt anyone feeling too defensive about it, but none of them felt that this was really necessary for their school.

The **fourth** thing to be sorted out was the question of annotation of the items as they were discussed and decisions were made about which aspects of which standards they represented. They already had an annotation sheet they used for items in the children's individual portfolios, and there seemed little point in change for the sake of it, so they kept the same one. You can see it on page 75 in Chapter Four. They decided it would be useful, too, to keep the 'Next steps' section, to focus on the next obvious step based on the work they were looking at, and to remind them again that the fundamental purpose of assessment is to improve teaching and learning, to feedforward not just feedback.

Marion had been to a few of these standardising sessions organised by the Local Education Authority and reminded the other Co-ordinators about the basics which made such a difference. "Make sure you've got enough tables", she said. "Take one item at a time, tidy up regularly or you'll get completely lost, and don't forget how important it is to specify the 'context' – the task from which this outcome has come, and the level of support given to the child. Give someone the job of keeping the group on task, helping people to make their contribution, keeping an eye on the time, drawing out the key points of the discussion and its conclusions and making sure items are properly annotated. It's a full-time job for someone, and means they may not be able to take much part in the discussion itself, but they are making an invaluable contribution in another way. "As it happened, Jane, the English Co-ordinator, played this 'facilitator' role herself in the first term, but then one of the younger teachers offered to do it for the Maths meetings and turned out to be brilliant at it: another incidental staff development opportunity which the Head added to her list.

Finally, they thought about what they would call this process. The Local Education Authority called it 'Agreement Trialling' but Marion felt that this name conjured up images that were neither very accurate nor very helpful. She always tried to avoid using the word 'evidence' to describe items or records which exemplified a standard or a judgement, and the use of the term 'trialling' had similar legalistic connotations. The Head wanted to keep the idea of 'standards', and they decided in the end on 'Sharing Standards' and vowed to avoid the use of acronyms. Why spend time on a name? Because what we call things does matter, and anyway it only took a few minutes.

Of course, things didn't work out exactly as expected. Audrey made a very positive contribution to the exercise once she was clear that it was purposeful and precise. Despite all the Science Co-ordinator's efforts, Science turned out to be really problematic, with people much more anxious and defensive about it than they were with English and Maths. What the exercise revealed was a general lack of confidence about some particular aspects of Science, which would become the focus of further staff development. The annotation sheet worked fine, but they adjusted the headings on it, adding some more specific prompts about the 'context'. They were so pleased with the outcomes of the English discussion that they used some of the items on a big display board at the next parents' meeting to show what was meant by a level, and what a wide range of attainment each level covered.

A further outcome was both unexpected and presented implications which are still being worked on. The Head of English from the neighbouring high school accepted the invitation to come to the standardising meeting. She was familiar with the exercise having been involved in English exams with school-based assessment. What was new was the insight she gained into the standards and tasks expected of pupils in the primary school, many of whom went on to become pupils at her school. She took this insight back with her and suggested that her Maths and Science colleagues might also find the experience illuminating, which they did. The high school offered some expertise and the loan of some resources in the troublesome aspects of Science. A display of some Maths investigations produced by Year 6 was mounted in the high school entrance hall, which delighted the children, pleased their teachers, and caused some discussion in the Maths department about whether the differentiation in the

Year 7 curriculum was sufficient to cater properly for a small group of mathematically gifted children they were about to 'inherit'. This was the first time that primary and secondary teachers had worked together discussing specific standards and their application to the work of children from both schools, and they found it more useful than some of the other shared activities they had been involved with. The Heads of both schools, and some of the other primary schools in the area, are now asking for some support from the LEA in doing some more. Watch this space.

The decision to focus on one 'subject' each term slowed the process down, but the Head was happy that the job was done well rather than quickly, and she felt there had been some very useful spin-off for the school from the strategy they'd adopted.

Key points

1. **Specifying standards can add precision to teaching and empower students. However, specifying standards can also fragment learning to an unproductive extent.**

2. **Some teachers may feel anxious about the greater accountability which specific standards can produce.**

3. **The first reason for standardising (i.e. pursuing consistency in the interpretation and application of standards) is to be fair to the pupils.**

4. **Standardising questions the professional autonomy of the individual teacher.**

5. **A 'standardising log' and a portfolio of annotated exemplars of agreed standards help both to improve consistency of judgement–making, and to provide evidence of your efforts to do so.**

One big question:

In the assessment of teaching competence, how would you define the standards to be applied?

Chapter Seven:
Student Involvement

If you've read this book from the beginning, or other things I've written over the years, you'll probably realise that involving students in learning and assessment is one of my continuing themes. Why? I'd like to be able to say that my conviction about the usefulness of student involvement in assessment sprang from my knowledge of the research findings on the issue, but I confess that it didn't. First and foremost I believe in involving learners in the assessment process because I myself have found it useful and effective, both as a learner and as a teacher. For me it's not a dogma, or an icon of 'political correctness': properly involving the learner improves learning, which is all the reason we need. Any other consequences of such involvement are a bonus. Beyond this conviction from personal experience, over recent years I have found research evidence from around the world which supports the involvement of students in the assessment process as part of effective learning.

So what's the rationale for student involvement? Certainly as an idea it is far from popular (initially) with many teachers, who regard the idea with some suspicion. It can be messy and unpredictable, and take time which could otherwise be spent on instruction. It might even be seen to reduce the teacher's control over the learning environment and thereby become part of a perceived conspiracy to undermine teachers' professional status. Even for the students the advantages of involvement are not necessarily self-evident. "Teachers are paid to teach," the students may say, " and deciding what's correct and what's not is part of that." It probably takes less effort to be told what to do than to be expected to take some part in the process, although learning by 'trial and error' can get tedious. Some students may not care about being successful in their education at school and beyond, but there are many more who do, recognising that such success improves their range of choices and gives them greater control over their own futures. At some point in our learning lives we need to become practically self-starting and self-motivating: this takes confidence and identifiable skills which have to be developed gradually over time. The process has to start in school, or autonomous effective learning will be achievable only by a fraction of those who need it.

Let us assume that all of us recognise the importance of helping students to become independent learners. Certainly words to this effect can be found in practically every set of school aims or 'mission statement'. If we are serious about achieving these stated aims we will consider strategies so to do. We do not expect that it will have a 'quick-fix' solution or require no effort on our part, or that the students will find it easy. We will apply our intelligence to the issue and make intelligent decisions, taking account of both the circumstances and consequences of certain courses of action. Learning autonomy may be the goal, but it will not be achieved merely by wishing it so.

As a start to working out what might be done to involve students progressively in their own learning, consider first what successful independent learning actually entails.

Pre-conditions for successful independent learning

- the learner believes that he/she is capable of learning;

- she knows enough about herself to set learning targets within her extended grasp;

- he is willing to make the effort and commitment;

- she is aware of different ways of tackling a learning task, and able to make good decisions depending on the circumstances;

- he has access to useful resources and knows how to use them;

- she is not afraid of failure and knows how to learn from it.

There are more, no doubt, but these will do for a start, serving to illustrate that they represent a combination of learned skills and attitudes which we cannot expect to develop unaided. They are definitely worth pursuing: think how our lives and our communities would be positively different if young people left our schools armed with these capabilities.

Philosophical conviction is one thing: making it work in the classroom is something else and the practicalities have to be considered carefully. The involvement of students in their learning provides a spectrum of possibilities, with direct involvement in assessment as part of this range. We already know that assessment is an integral part of teaching and learning. It will come as no surprise to learn that involvement in learning means involvement in assessment and vice versa. Going back to the original cycle of teaching and learning which we've already looked at, here are some questions about the balance of involvement between teachers and students.

1. Who decides what is to be taught and learned, and on what basis?

2. Who determines the starting point in this learning?

3. Who decides how learning is to be organised, and the methods to be used?

4. Who provides, articulates and exemplifies the criteria by which success will be judged?

5. Who does the assessment, and how?

6. Who records the outcomes, where, how and when?

To answer each of these questions there are choices to be made along a continuum. At one end of the continuum the answer in each case is 'The teacher'. At the other end of the continuum the answer is 'The learner'. Different points on the continuum could be chosen to answer different questions, although it is unlikely that the two extremes would be in use simultaneously with the same group of learners. Teachers may have personal preferences, just as they have in choices about teaching style, but their overriding concern is to meet the needs of learners rather than themselves. Often both teacher and students face

TINA, CHENISE, DONNA, CLINT, SIT DOWN, PLEASE. THIS USE OF THE SEMI-COLON IN MIDDLE ENGLISH IS FASCINATING...

together the demands of an externally prescribed teaching programme, but even within that there's more room for choice and learner involvement than is sometimes recognised.

Taking one of the questions above as an example, how would the spectrum of possibilities work out? Question 3 deals directly with the establishment of criteria by which the success of learning will be judged. At one extreme these criteria will be decided by the teacher without reference at all to the learners. They might also be kept secret by the teachers both before and even after the assessment event. All that the learners might hope for is a result.

At the other end of the spectrum, what could happen? Here the students would examine the given learning task and its objectives which were presumably known to them, and decide the basis on which successful achievement of these objectives might be ascertained. The question of who was then to apply these criteria and make the assessment judgement could be decided separately. It is perfectly possible for the criteria to be decided by the students and the judgement made by the teacher, and equally possible for the criteria to be decided entirely by the teacher, shared with the students and the assessment then done by the students themselves. All such decisions will depend on the relevant variables, the ultimate purpose being to improve the students' learning through their understanding and application of standards.

> *A young friend told me how their University exam.*
> *results were issued. The students were given a time*
> *and a place where their results would be displayed.*
> *They gathered in anxious groups by the wall in the*
> *question. At the given time a university official*
> *appeared and pinned onto the wall a long list of*
> *names. If your name was on the list you had passed:*
> *if it was not you had failed and would either have to*
> *retake the whole exam or leave the course. A great*

> *crush ensued as people tried to read the list. If you did*
> *not see your name straight away you stayed longer*
> *in the crush to scour the list again. Occasionally*
> *someone struggled out of the crush in tears. The only*
> *justification offered for this procedure was that it had*
> *always been done this way.*

For each of the six questions there is a teacher-dominated answer at one end of the spectrum of possibilities, a student-dominated answer at the other end, and a range of shared answers in the middle. Use your common sense and experience to work out the possible courses of action, and the practical consequences of the decisions you might make. If you want to move towards more student involvement, you would need to take account of your own starting point as well as theirs and probably take things one step at a time.

Involvement in reviewing learning in the classroom

There is nothing special about the techniques we can use for involving learners in reviewing in the classroom. What is special is the belief that this process actually helps learning and is therefore taken seriously, given time and thought. Sometimes when teachers start to involve pupils in this way they try to make it very structured, and use the same structure every time, leading to review feeling like something extra added on rather than something integral to the classroom. There are a variety of structures you can use, and it really helps to mix them up, just as you would with teaching styles, to keep the students interested and to give each of them the chance to work occasionally in the way they prefer.

- One method is to discuss with each student individually his or her work, its strengths and difficulties, and ways forward. There is no doubt that the individual attention alone will boost the interest and motivation of the student: the quality of your questions and their responses is an added bonus. Marking or grading work with the student is an excellent way of achieving clear relevant feedback and the feeling of central involvement, but it is very time-consuming, especially for the secondary teacher who sees so many students. It's worth trying to see individual students, even though it may be only once in a long time. Some students can go through school having never experienced such one-to-one attention for more than a few seconds, and it's something all of them deserve. Involving students in reviewing does not mean, in my experience at least, that this needs to be one-to-one all the time: it's just part of a wider repertoire.

- Children can review their work in a small group, just as they work in this way from time to time. They will need some ground rules to do this successfully, of course, and the groups will need to be organised so that they feel comfortable offering and receiving constructive criticism as well as specific positive feedback.

- Reviewing in a pair is also very helpful. In some classes children have partners with whom they work regularly, and this structure can be extended to include peer marking and reviewing.

- Much excellent teaching happens with the group all together, led by their teacher, and whole-group reviewing can be very effective too. Using her skill to make herself understood to a variety of learners simultaneously, the teacher asks questions and prompts the class to think and talk about their work, both collectively and individually. The outcomes, in terms of the students' next steps recorded in their folders or work books, may be slightly different for each of them, but the process was explored for all of them at once. Of course there's nothing new about this: teachers have been talking to students about their work since teaching began, but a more considered and systematic approach can make a good idea work even better.

So the structures for classroom reviewing are several and varied. What about the prompts we can give to generate the quality of reflection we are looking for?

These questions are used in one form or another in countless classrooms already. I've seen them used with 8–year–olds and 18–year–olds. I remember showing them once to staff at a sixth form college, who claimed that their students weren't mature enough to deal with them, but I think that said more about the teachers than the students.

Prompts for reviewing in the classroom

1. What have you **done** during this topic/lesson/unit/ module/week?

2. What have you **enjoyed**? Why?

3. What have you **found difficult**? Why?

4. What do you think you've **learned** during the topic?

5. What would you show as **evidence** of what you've learned?

6. In the next topic/lesson etc. what are you going to focus on to continue what's been successful, and to improve what needs to be improved? What are your **next steps**?

Working towards greater student involvement in the assessment process

As a secondary school teacher myself I thought for some years that involvement in the assessment process would probably not be possible until pupils reached adolescence. I've no idea where that particular prejudice came from, but it's been shown to be faulty time and again by my work over the past decade with teachers of younger children. (Maybe that says something about the way I was trained to teach.) Even in the nursery school, many teachers encourage children to make choices about their activities and to reflect on what they have been doing. If we can use the right level of language and ideas, reflecting on the experience and the outcomes of learning can be effective from the early years of the primary school. "Did you enjoy that activity?" is a regular question. Whatever the answer, be it "Yes" or "No", add the further question "Why?" or "Why not?" and the assessment process has begun. Focus the learner, or yourself, on the future with a further question about "What would you do differently next time?" and we have entered the realm of assessment for learning.

Let me offer some real examples of learners at various ages becoming involved in assessment for learning.

The 6-year-old

Alana is asked by her teacher to choose one picture from her folder which she is particularly pleased with, to show to her next teacher. Having made her choice, the teacher asks her why she has chosen this particular one. Alana explains that she likes the colours she has used, and that the birds in the sky look like proper birds. Why is that? Because there are some big ones and some small ones. The teacher writes this down for her on a little slip of paper to go with the picture in Alana's achievement folder.

Joe is doing Reading Recovery. He sits next to his tutor and reads to her. When he makes a mistake she doesn't correct it for him, but asks him instead to correct it for himself. She waits while he thinks, and prompts him to look at the rest of the sentence. She waits again, he corrects himself, she congratulates him and he carries on.

The 9–year–old

Shahida and two of her friends are working together on a project to find out about geysers. Other groups are finding out about other aspects of thermal and volcanic activity, and they will each present their findings to the whole group, in the form of a display and a brief oral report. Before they start the whole group discuss the kinds of things they will need to do, both in the research and the presentation of their work. They decide on four key things they will need to be aware of and that they will be judged on:

- how they organise things to make sure that everybody makes a contribution and that the job is completed properly and on time;

- the range and variety of places they look for information;

- how clearly they understand and can explain how a geyser actually works;

- the accuracy and neatness of their written work and diagrams.

Having decided these important things, the teacher writes them up on a big sheet of paper and puts them on the wall so that they are not forgotten. They also decide that their work will be assessed as follows:

- the group itself will keep track of how they organised themselves, and give themselves a mark out of 10 for sharing the work out and finishing on time;

- the rest of the class will give the group a mark out 10 for the clarity of their explanation;

- the teacher will give each group a mark out of 10 for the range of information they have used, and for the accuracy of their written work.

After this assessment, each group will discuss what each group member needs to do to make their work better next time, write these targets at the back of their project folders, and make sure they remember them. The teacher will look at all these so that she can remind them too.

A few weeks later, towards the end of a topic on the Roman army, the teacher explains the test she is going to give them in order to check how much they understand and remember of what they have learned. She explains how the test will be arranged, and what kinds of things she is looking for. She gives them all a sample question to do, and then asks them to look at each other's work in pairs and see if they have done what she asked them to do. They work out together what each of them has done well, and what they need to do better. The next day they do the proper test, using what they learned from the sample exercise to help do a better job. The teacher marks the test, and they spend a few minutes talking through how it turned out.

The 14–year–old

In Mike's Technology class the teacher always starts each new chunk of work by explaining what they're going to do, where it connects with what they've done before, and what specifically she wants them to be able to do by the time they've finished it.

She always checks too whether any of them have done anything similar before, at another school or at home, and what they can remember about it. At the end of the activity both Mike and the teacher fill in an assessment record which has the teacher's criteria down the side and room for comments from each of them about different aspects of the work. Mike fills the sheet in first, trying to be specific about what he's learned and what he's had trouble with. The teacher adds any further or different comments she wants to make. Both of them have to suggest a least one specific next step to improve Mike's work. The sheets are kept in Mike's Technology folder so that both he and his teacher can refer to them. He can show them to his parents too when he takes the folder home.

The 17–year–old

Maria is just starting the second year of an Advanced Level English course. It took her a while in the previous year to understand and adjust to the different expectations of the Advanced Level. For a few months her teacher had to offer lots of guidance and structure for the written work, but increasingly now the teacher is expecting the group to be involved in working out the criteria and expected standards for the tasks he set for them. They had discussed the stated expectations in the 'syllabus' and what it would look like generally if they were to meet these standards. Now they had to apply these general expectations to a particular task, working out the mark scheme for the piece. When they'd completed the piece, they would each 'mark' their own work, and then choose one or two to be looked at by the whole group. These 'marks' would not count towards their final exam grade, but the feedback they got from this way of working was making a positive difference to their performance, which would in turn produce higher results in the formal assignments and the final exam. The students had wanted a lot of teacher guidance originally, and got it, but now they appreciated the chance to work things out for themselves. Some of those in the group who were also doing vocational courses recognised this way of working, and were accustomed to being given greater responsibility for their own learning and assessment.

The 47-year-old

Ruth is learning how to write books. She knows she wants to communicate some ideas, and has to work out what characteristics she is aiming for in the final product. Not too much jargon, plenty of headings, examples whenever they would be useful, key points at the end of each chapter, not too long – all of these are on her list. So she writes, thinking as she does about her own standards and whether they are being met. They may not be the right criteria for everyone, but they're important to her. From the first book she learned how to set about it, the order in which to do things, how long various stages would take, how much planning was needed before she started to write a full chapter, and so on. She's on her own with it, but she believes in her capacity to learn, knows her own weak points and how to cope with them, doesn't get too discouraged when things don't work out first time, and keeps going. Next she wants to write fiction, so she is going to get some expert help because this is a new skill.

Feelings are facts: how do we feel about involving students?

So far in this chapter we've looked at the rationale for student involvement in the assessment process, the necessary pre-conditions, some structures and prompts, and how the level of support might change as learners develop from childhood to adulthood. There's nothing very difficult involved, except the management of time, but the ways people feel can produce failure, or reluctance even to start the process off. The feelings of the three key parties involved – teachers, students and parents – will differ, and all need to be examined.

Teachers will obviously have concerns about how much time and organisation it may take to achieve effective learner involvement in the assessment process. For some teachers however the anxiety goes a little deeper. By making a deliberate effort to open up the assessment process they may feel that they are losing control of the ultimate judgement of the quality of learning, which has maintained until now a comfortable distance between themselves and their students. Some believe that sharing assessment standards and inviting students to join in will be the thin end of a highly undesirable wedge, at the end of which students are calling you by your first name and putting their feet on your desk. Keeping control of the assessment process is a way of keeping control of the students, and loss of control is to be avoided at all costs. In a sense the argument is sound. If student involvement is interpreted to mean handing over the assessment process to the students and leaving them to it then one might share the concern. But as we have seen, decisions about involving students can be made sensibly and progressively, starting at an early age with plenty of structure and gradually extending the range of student responsibility. The teacher trains and encourages, with the prime purpose being to improve both the quality of learning and the preparation of the student for future learning.

A further worry among some teachers about the process is actually about the added sense of accountability which results from opening up the assessment standards to scrutiny by students and others. Student involvement is only a minor feature of this scenario, which is inevitable as soon as specific standards are published. Greater accountability will inevitably follow, and the involvement of students might actually be productive by helping students to understand the complexities of the assessment process.

The best approach to these anxieties is to encourage open discussion about them: the answer to them will depend on the particular combination of feelings about management, workload, control or accountability. In any event, if a teacher does want to involve students more he or she will take it one step at a time, opening up the criteria, sharing them with the learners, offering more specific feedback, providing opportunities for review, just keeping going so long as learning is improving and both teacher and students feel comfortable.

For **students** the anxieties may be completely different, but just as varied. Some students just don't want to be more responsible for their own learning, in the same way as they may be uncomfortable about accepting other adult responsibilities, preferring to remain dependent. For a start it's easier to blame someone else for your failure to learn than it is to blame yourself. Other students may feel that they haven't been involved enough, and fret under the externality of the assessment process which has such an impact on their lives. Others again may want greater involvement but feel unsupported in learning how to achieve it successfully. There is another feeling you catch sight of from time to time, in talking to the students themselves and also to their teachers who know them well. Students who are younger or less confident, or even more distrustful of adults, can feel intimidated if the teacher tries to focus on them too intently. For these students the chance to be part of a small self-chosen group may be preferable to the one-to-one with an adult. Or it may be fruitful to offer the chance to review performance with an older student, who can be very helpful to prompt reflection and target-setting but is not such an authority figure as the teacher. At this point assessment for motivation overlaps with a system of mentoring, a connection which has great potential and needs exploring further.

Some years ago, working in the inner city, I talked to a young man who was part of a pilot scheme on

> *student involvement in assessment. It was clear that this was possibly the first time in his life when an interested adult had talked to him individually about his learning and his needs. His first worry was that this had something to do with the probation service. Why else would someone be so interested in him? He found the conversation difficult, even though he was talking to a teacher he knew well and respected. Half way through the review he got up and left. Asked why later, he responded that the teacher had been "mugging his mind". It was an expression I have never forgotten, and it reminds me that our young people deserve a proper explanation of any new procedure we offer them, and that they have the right to find their own way through it. It is just not enough to say, "Trust us, this will be good for you".*

As with the feelings of teachers, there is no one strategy which can accommodate such a variety of responses, all of which are legitimate and spring from our varying personalities and experiences. The decisions which we make about methods of involvement must depend on the starting point of the students and what exactly they need to overcome their doubts. Experience of helping schools to achieve greater student involvement tells me that the devil is often in the detail rather than the principle. The same review process used too often can be just boring, and it is irritating to be expected to be involved if no-one has explained the reason and what's in it for you. Sometimes the most effective way to encourage older students to become involved for the first time is to have the reasons presented to them by someone who isn't a school teacher but an employer in the local community, or a person working with young people in higher education who knows the importance of being a more independent learner.

The best way to encourage effective involvement is to expect it from an early age and make it part of normal learning activity, using techniques appropriate to particular needs and circumstances, rather than bolting it on as something separate. There is an issue here for whole-school approaches: in the primary school as the child moves from one class teacher to the next it is important that the opportunity for involvement is continued, rather than encouraged one year and closed down the next. In the secondary school, as the student moves from one teacher to the next, the chosen techniques of involvement may – and should – vary to reflect the particular learning context, but the opportunity continues. Good assessment at any age and in any learning area needs a range of methods, each fitted to a clear purpose: involving the learner is part of that full range.

The views of **parents** need to be considered too if we are to involve students more. Just as many students believe assessment to be the teacher's job not theirs, so too do many of their parents. They deserve a clear rationale, to understand that such involvement is a genuine effort to raise learning standards, not an abdication of the teacher's responsibility. They too may need to hear about the benefits from those who offer young people jobs and further training and education, as well as from the teachers themselves. The most powerful and convincing exponents of the benefits of involvement can be the students who have experienced a well-planned programme. If research evidence about the impact of effective involvement on learning would help allay parental fears about their children being subject to some trendy experimentation, then the research evidence could be shared too. These ideas are not new in education but parents may feel that they are: they deserve both information and reassurance, as a change in approach is introduced, not afterwards. This is especially true if the school is proposing changes in the way pupils' written work is marked. The outcomes of such changes may be visible in the pupils' work books and folders as they go between home and school, and parents should not find out about change accidentally. Here again, if the pupils themselves

147

understand the rationale they are the best ambassadors for the school, after some initial explanation has been offered directly to parents.

Key points

1. Involving learners in the assessment process is about small, progressive steps taken sensibly by teachers in the pursuit of more effective learning.

2. Begin to train and encourage children to be involved at an early age, and keep going.

3. A wide range of strategies and possibilities is available, requiring appropriate decisions and use of a variety of techniques.

4. Feelings about the idea of student involvement are sometimes deep-rooted: they need to be discussed honestly and seriously, and acted upon if necessary.

One big question:

At what ages or stages do children become 'ready' for various levels of involvement in their own assessment?

Chapter Eight:
'Value-added'

So far this book has been largely devoted to the principles and mechanics of connecting assessment and learning. There are three other areas I would like to look at briefly, just to provoke some further thinking, and to ask questions rather than provide answers. The first of these is the topical pursuit of 'value-added' as a measure of school effectiveness in achieving improved learning for its pupils.

The use of the term seems to denote that 'value' can in fact be 'measured' both at the start and the end of the child or the cohort's school career, the first number subtracted from the second and some meaningful information derived from the result. No one could deny the importance of investigating the effectiveness of a school system which absorbs large amounts of public funding, but the notion that this can be done by the application of a simple mathematical formula is a myth which still seems to linger with some of our politicians. Measuring the output of a school is not as easy as measuring the output of a factory. Why not?

The first problem is the need to agree what we believe is the purpose of the school. Sometimes it appears that the most valuable of our aspirations are the least visible and hardest to quantify, while the easiest to measure may not be the most important or tell the whole story. Also, crucially, it is notoriously difficult to disentangle the myriad factors which appear to affect a child's learning, many of which are beyond the control of the school – or at least subject to out-of-school influences. In the anti-professional climate which has been a feature of recent decades in the United Kingdom, the debate about value-added has been muddied by the dismissal of such complexities as examples of teachers' defensiveness. While the research work and the argument continues, the best one can do is present some of the possibilities, recognising their flaws and hoping that more progress will soon be made.

At a national level, using whatever reliable information is available, it may at some point be possible, for example, to use National Curriculum level data to examine the value added by a school or schools between the end of Key Stage One (at age 7) and the end of successive key stages. Level data so far, however, is both crude and of questionable reliability, which could undermine the usefulness of the exercise as well as being unfair to some schools and their pupils. Public examination results are also widely used, compared with standardised data about the child on entry to the secondary school, to check whether children do actually achieve what we might predict for them. This exercise too needs to take account of other factors, some of which – parental occupation for example – are both apparently important and contentious. Some school systems have undertaken useful work investigating the possible models which could be used, but no nationally satisfactory process has yet emerged.

In the absence of national guidance on the matter, there is room still for individual schools to find their own way through, if they have the energy and the expertise to do so. Certainly it's a challenging question to ask: teachers, of all people, should be intensely curious about the difference they make to children over the number of years the child may spend in a school. A start could be made by re-examining what the school states to be its aims and aspirations for its pupils. These will include some clearly 'investigateable' things, such as pupils' fulfilment of their academic potential – so long as we can find a way of measuring that potential. It's much harder to check some of our other aspirations – preparation for adult life, for example, or the development of moral values, or increased motivation.

As schools are increasingly involved in development planning, it is likely that there will be a steady improvement in the practice of connecting these plans to the overall stated aims of the school, and then building into the plan the means of checking that targets have actually been achieved. Some of this checking will involve examining the outcomes of learning, which brings us back once more to the accuracy, relevance and reliability of the school's assessment procedures, both external and internal. A proper school-based investigation of value-added, proceeding from the school's definition of 'value', will then involve some well-planned activities over a number of years, monitoring children as they move through the school.

Such monitoring could be, and is, conducted through periodic screening, of reading for example, which could be used both diagnostically for individual children and as 'pointers to further enquiry' about trends or anomalies which the data appear to reveal. The use of well-chosen and appropriate standardised tests could be valuable here, but with care so that the cost in both money and time was properly justified by the use made of the results. Investigations of value-added could be qualitative as well as quantitative, focusing on a wider range of learning outcomes than those which can most easily be tested. The children could be presented each year with a task designed to generate certain outcomes which could then be compared year by year to see what progression in learning had actually occurred. Here again, the worth of the exercise would depend on what was done with the information generated by it.

Other schools have begun to conduct very close scrutiny of the development of a small but representative sample of a year group, followed throughout their school careers. Through focusing on a smaller number of children more searching questions could be asked, of the children and their parents as well as the teachers and the pupils' tangible 'output'. This arrangement could certainly reveal a wider range of information, in line with the comprehensive aspirations espoused by the school. Making such a process work effectively is a long-term commitment. It has to be based on fundamental aims agreed by the school and its community which are unlikely to change radically over a number of years. The school's procedures need to survive changes in personnel and resist short-term bandwagons which regularly roll past. The information revealed by such scrutiny would need to be considered regularly by teachers, managers, parents, governors and trustees.

It is no surprise that value-added has generated much discussion and little discernible action over the past few years. The issues involved are difficult both philosophically and technically. Furthermore, to do the job properly schools need to think, plan and gather data over the long term, when everything else happening around them seems to driven by short-term considerations. This dilemma is not unique to education. As the twentieth century nears its end the old certainties seem to crumble with ever-increasing speed, and planning ahead seems more and more futile. Slowly we learn to come terms with continuing uncertainty, to the point where we can recognise those elements of our aspirations which will sustain through change, and be willing to invest time in both adding value and checking that we have done so.

School Improvement

School Improvement may be the issue of the decade, but the capital letters should not be taken to denote anything radically new. Rather we are being urged to focus on the fundamentals of effective teaching and learning as the heart of the improvement process, with as much rigour, thought and systematic self-scrutiny as we can muster. At the end of the day, however, there are no quick-fix solutions, and a successful strategy in one school may not work so well in another, because of the host of complex variables involved.

If teaching and learning are at the heart of school improvement, and assessment is at the heart of effective teaching and learning, which I believe to be true, then a school's approach to assessment is of central importance to its development. Never was it more important than now to remember the principles on which such assessment should be based. Sound assessment has to be:

- purposeful and planned;

- based on clear objectives;

- designed to allow each learner to show what s/he knows;

- fair and free of bias;

- consistent and reliable;

- manageable, aiming for quality rather than quantity of data;

- used to improve both teaching and learning.

Only when these principles apply will the information generated by the process be good enough to underpin the school improvement process. For sustainable continuing improvement in the classroom, every teacher needs to both understand and be able to act upon these principles: assessment after all is not a periodic additional duty for teachers but an integral part of what we do, all the time. The teacher's confidence and skills in this area will have a major impact on the daily classroom experience of all our pupils. A growing body of research findings has already generated some conclusions about the features of schools which are sustaining steady improvement. One such conclusion is that school improvement cannot be driven entirely from the 'top' of the school. Classroom teachers are central to effective change, working within a climate which encourages and values the highest quality of teaching from day to day. In such a climate, all teachers regard themselves as learners, and accept their measure of responsibility for the development of the whole school. This being true, the professional training and development of teachers in assessment should be high on our agenda, both pre-service and in-service. In particular, what does such training offer about assessment as part of teaching and learning?

Teacher education and assessment

Teacher education is a combination of two stages, pre-service and in-service. At the pre-service stage, which is increasingly rushed as more and more aspects of teaching jostle to be included in reduced time, the importance of assessment is twofold. Firstly, assessment principles need to be taught and learned like any other part of the training; secondly, that training itself needs to be assessed. My own guess is that trainee teachers take with them into the classroom not what they have been taught about assessment, but what they have experienced themselves, both at school and in their training. The key question, therefore, is whether the principles of sound assessment outlined above are actually applied to the assessment of trainee teachers. Does the assessment experience they encounter model the best practice to which they aspire in their own teaching? If not, why not, and what needs to be done to close this gap between rhetoric and reality?

I ask these questions drawing on personal and anecdotal evidence of which one should always be wary. I know very little about the assessment of trainee teachers because I have spent the least thirteen years working with serving teachers, some of whom were trained decades ago when assessment was treated differently. Others of my clients were trained more recently, but that training did not necessarily enable them to understand the basic principles of assessment, or to apply them on a daily basis in their marking and other feedback to their pupils. Some teachers trained within the last five years seem to have been offered practical techniques for the management of the current requirements of National Curriculum assessment, but not enough understanding to know how to adapt their techniques when requirements change. At a time of rapid change, therefore, newly-qualified teachers may need further training almost immediately, which has to be provided by the school at its own expense.

Obviously, teaching effectively is a highly complex affair which cannot be properly trained for in the very short time available, particularly for postgraduate trainees. Some prioritisation of focus at pre-service training must take place, whether that training is based in a higher education institution or a school. Perhaps all trainee secondary teachers are encouraged to consider, discuss and practise effective 'marking' before they encounter their first pile of books. Perhaps all trainee teachers, in all phases, are expected to analyse the purpose and audience of different forms of record-keeping, so that they can make good choices when they have the chance to do so. Perhaps all our newly-qualified teachers do emerge from training with these experiences but have to set their questions and ideas aside when faced with the intractable systems already in place in the schools in which they are now teaching. Perhaps they have experienced themselves some of the methods which might be useful in school, but they have been unimpressed by them and disinclined to inflict them on others. Who knows? I admit that I do not know the answers to these questions, but I still feel the need to ask them. If you are yourself currently training for your first teaching job, reflect on what you are learning about assessment as part of the teaching and learning cycle, and on how you are being assessed. What conclusions do you come to?

In-service teacher education

If my understanding of pre-service education suffers from my own ignorance of it, I suspect that my insights into in-service may suffer from being too close to it, and only really knowing about what I provide myself. For what it's worth, my own experience has led me to some conclusions about what constitutes effective in-service education on assessment matters.

1. No matter how sophisticated the task, it's worth asking regularly the **fundamental assessment questions:** "Why are we doing this assessment, and who is it for? Does what we actually do, or propose to do, match with this purpose and audience?"

2. Assessment seems to be riddled with jargon and esoteric language which needs to be explained clearly or not used

at all. For some reason, many teachers and parents seem to feel that assessment is 'hard', like Physics. This impression may be a myth, but it's tenacious, and we need to use **plain language** and specific examples to achieve clarity and raise confidence.

3. It helps to consider a wide range of possible assessment techniques, in terms of their purpose, their relevance, and their specific technical and management implications. Pooling and sharing ideas and experience can be very useful, as long as we are encouraged to analyse as well as narrate what we do.

4. It is important to encourage teachers to adopt a **balanced** approach to both teaching and assessment, and to avoid reliance on all–embracing theories.

5. We need to **understand about how children learn** if we are to be able to use assessment to assist learning. Information and investigations about theories of learning and motivation may seem to be a long way from assessment but they are entirely pertinent and can be a very productive place to start.

6. Any work with adults needs to appeal to a wide range of learning styles, just as it would with children. As assessment is so closely linked to teaching, in which many in-service clients are already highly experienced, it's also essential to start with and build on that experience rather than discount or ignore it. Be prepared to design your training programme from the expressed wants as well as the needs of the group. With potentially contentious issues like assessment, in my experience, fixed programmes, however slick, do not work well with teachers, who may suspect that their genuine concerns are being squeezed out of the structure.

7. Some experiential work, introduced with a clear rationale and well-handled, can be extremely effective in challenging

assumptions, encouraging insights and making them more memorable. It's worth remembering, however, that many of us have strong feelings about assessment rooted in our own childhood experiences, and these need to be handled carefully if we ask colleagues to recall and articulate them.

8. Different subject areas do attract different ways of thinking and different approaches to assessment. We can enjoy this diversity and learn from it, in the secondary school particularly, rather than insisting on identical assessment practice across the school. A balance can be found between subject autonomy and whole-school consistency.

9. Many assessment issues encountered in in-service education are actually more about management than assessment, and need to be dealt with as such. Identifying purposes, finding consensus and standardising, communicating with parents and others beyond the school, managing change – all these are encountered every day in training on assessment and have to be welcomed not brushed to one side. Technical understanding alone will not improve assessment practice in our schools.

Key Points

1. **The publication of raw outcomes of schooling reveal very little about the effectiveness of the school.**

2. **The investigation of 'value' must encompass qualitative as well as quantitative data.**

3. **School improvement has at its heart the improvement of teaching and learning, with effective assessment essential to both.**

4. **School improvement requires the active involvement of every teacher.**

5. Trainee teachers need to encounter the principles of effective assessment not just as something they learn but also as something they experience.

One big question:

How do we ensure and monitor excellent continuing professional development for all teachers?

Looking to the Future

Predicting the future in any area of our lives would be a folly. All one can do is look at current trends and extrapolate them somewhat to gain an impression of what we might expect to have in place five or ten years down the track. The only thing we can be sure of is that uncertainty is here to stay ! Those of us who prefer things to stay as they are have had an uncomfortable few years and are hopefully learning by now to accept uncertainty as part of life and to welcome rather than fear its impact upon us. We can reduce our craving for certainty without abandoning our values or the moral structure of our lives.

Some of the images in my crystal ball look remarkably familiar, at least for the next decade or so, while other parts of the picture have changed almost beyond recognition, mainly through the impact of technology which has been developing around us and is now close to reaching inside our schools, for teachers as well as for pupils.

Some current assessment phenomena seemed destined to stick around for a while. The development of explicit standards against which assessment will take place seems inexorable, unless the process is taken too far and collapses under its own weight. These public and specific standards are having and will continue to have inevitable consequences for all those involved with the educative process. Not only will assessment be designed to find evidence of the attainment of set standards, but the public nature of the exercise opens up the secret garden of judgement to learners and others. For the first time in the United Kingdom, that I know of, the marked scripts of national tests were returned to schools in 1995, a bold step which caused a furore, and some speculation about the accuracy and reliability of other external examinations which are still protected by public ignorance. As tests and examinations become based on specific standards rather than normative comparisons the mystique of assessment may begin to crumble, public scrutiny will increase, and once this particular Pandora's box has been opened I doubt whether the lid can be forced back on again. Specificity and accountability are here to stay, for a while at least, with all the implications they bring with them.

Another continuing trend appears to be the insistence on 'value-for-money' scrutiny of schools, and a systematic approach to school improvement. At least in the United Kingdom, an interesting political consensus appears to have emerged, which is likely to remain for the rest of this decade if not beyond. There will be changes of emphasis, obviously, but radical changes of direction are less likely than what we have witnessed over the past fifteen years. As we have discussed earlier, there are close links between assessment and school improvement, as the former provides much of the data to fuel the latter. This connection should reinforce both.

Developments in technology

Technology buffs will know far more than me about what awaits us, but I'm aware of how slowly technology has really taken root in many of our schools, and that there will have to be powerful incentives and some unprecedented investment if some of the available technologies will actually emerge into common use. I'm also aware that 'toys' can be seductive: they look as if they can improve education just by being there, which is far from true. The old saying, 'Rubbish in, rubbish out' needs to be writ large on our walls before we succumb to computerised record-keeping, reporting, or anything else which relies on the quality of the human decisions at the heart of the process.

Another awareness was brought home to me recently at an international assessment conference. The man from Singapore was asking for advice on appropriate assessment methods for learning by interactive video linked to a computer. It was a genuine question, and was met with a sigh from the man from Central Africa, who said they would be happy to have a computer in every school, never mind one for every student. One's priorities are affected by one's starting point, and there are gross inequalities in educational provision around the world which put some of this discussion about the use of technology in perspective.

Nevertheless, some of the new technologies are here and are already to be seen in our schools, in the United Kingdom and in North America. The hand–held computer into which the teacher feeds her observations of children's learning as they happen is already in use in the United States. It allows the teacher's information to be sorted, structured, and printed easily and instantly. I have a battery-powered hand-held computer of my own which serves as a diary, database and word processor: even I can see how the same technology could be adapted to meet daily assessment and record-keeping needs in school, without having teachers queue to enter information into static machines.

The possibilities of CD ROM and the Internet for teacher education, shared planning and standardising are extraordinary. Pursuing consistency in the interpretation and use of shared specific standards could be achieved effectively without teachers having to leave their own schools. It might be less fun, and the start up costs would be heavy, but standardising is already an expensive process, and in less populated areas with fewer schools further apart E-mail could revolutionise teacher to teacher communication. Already schools in various parts of the world where the necessary technology is available are linking up to provide a broader shared curriculum for all their students: the next step is to use those same systems for the purposes of assessment as well as teaching and learning.

Forward to fundamentals

As visions of the future go, mine are pretty mundane. I may be completely outpaced by developments over the next ten years, or the school in 2005 may handle assessment and record-keeping in exactly the same way as in 1995. No matter where the technology may take us, I still believe there is a central place in the teaching and learning process for the teacher – with all our frailty, unreliability, inefficiency, humanity. Assessment is not now and never will be an absolute science, no matter how much sophisticated technology is brought to bear. The technology may help, but the design of learning and the judgement of its effectiveness will remain a person-based process for a while yet. The fundamentals of sound assessment will prevail, and with them the empowerment of both teachers and learners to make assessment serve learning, not the other way round.

Conclusion

All the key points from the ends of the chapters are listed below, with the hope that you will be inspired to delve back to the main text if you haven't already read it. The 'big questions' are repeated too, just to remind us that they are still around, and still interesting.

Chapter One

1. Start the curriculum planning process with a shared view of the 'big picture', for the whole school or for a 'key stage'.

2.. Find an acceptable balance between the 'tight' plan, which may not be responsive to children's needs, and the 'loose' plan which lacks any sense of direction.

3. Deciding on learning objectives and expected learning outcomes is an essential part of planning for assessment.

4.. Share these objectives and expectations with your pupils.

One big question:
When does curriculum entitlement become curriculum prescription?

Chapter Two

1. Differentiation is about trying to ensure that the right pupils get the right tasks.

2.. We need to find out, think and talk about the factors which affect the way children learn, and the way they show what they know.

3. Through sound assessment we discover the pupil's learning needs: then we need access to a wide enough range of materials, resources and ideas to meet those needs as far as we can. When teachers share their materials, resources and ideas each of them has a wider repertoire to choose from.

4. A teacher's preferred learning style will probably affect her/his teaching style: with care we can become as aware of the pupils' needs as we are of our own teaching 'comfort'.

One big question:
Which is more important – to give each child
the best chance to show what he knows, or
to be fair to all children by treating them all
the same?

Chapter Three

1. Progression = Differentiation + Communication + Professional Respect.

2. If it were easy we would have managed it more successfully by now.

3. Where shared specific standards are used, common across age ranges or key stages, a level is a level is a level, no matter which age or stage it arose from.

4. Progression 'records' are probably the least useful of all the progression strategies, but seem to absorb the most teacher time and attention.

One big question:
Why are some teachers so dismissive of
children's previous learning?

Chapter Four

1. Marking involves daily assessment, feedback to learners and record–keeping for ourselves. For many teachers it is extremely time-consuming and needs to be rigorously reviewed.

2. The use of codes and grades for feedback is of very limited help in improving learning unless all those involved know precisely what the grades mean.

3. When pupils are trained to be effective 'markers' of each other's and their own work, their involvement can be advantageous for both them and their teachers.

4. Record–keeping systems should be determined by the information they are designed to accommodate, not the other way round.

5. Effective marking–records need context, focus and feedforward.

6. Marking for expected outcomes in the product of pupils' learning must be complemented by some systematic observation of pupils as individuals, in order to spot unexpected and significant learning.

One big question:
What is the maximum time which should
ever elapse between work being done and
feedback being received by the learner?

Chapter Five

1.   A 'portfolio' is just a place where we keep examples of a pupil's work.

2.   The crucial questions in selecting what goes in a portfolio are 'Why and who for?'

3.   Consider how to keep the minimum number of items which will serve the needs of the maximum number of purposes and audiences.

4.   Developing subject/standards–based portfolios can generate really good discussion about learning, tasks and expectations, if it's well managed.

**One big question:
Is an achievement portfolio for every child
really worth the time and effort (and storage
space) it takes to produce?**

Chapter Six

1.   Specifying standards can add precision to teaching and empower students. However, specifying standards can also fragment learning to an unproductive extent.

2.   Some teachers may feel anxious about the greater accountability which specific standards can produce.

3.   The first reason for standardising (i.e. pursuing consistency in the interpretation and application of standards) is to be fair to the pupils.

4.   Standardising questions the professional autonomy of the individual teacher.

5.   A 'standardising log' and portfolio of annotated exemplars of agreed standards help both to improve consistency of judgement–making, and to provide evidence of your efforts to do so.

One big question:
In the assessment of teaching competence,
how would you define the standards to be
applied?

Chapter Seven

1.   Involving learners in the assessment process is about small, progressive steps taken sensibly by teachers in the pursuit of more effective learning.

2.   Begin to train and encourage children to be involved at an early age, and keep going.

3.   A wide range of strategies and possibilities is available, requiring appropriate decisions to use of a variety of techniques.

4.   Feelings about the idea of student involvement are sometimes deep-rooted: they need to be discussed honestly and seriously, and acted upon if necessary.

One big question:
At what ages or stages do children become
'ready' for various levels of involvement in
their own assessment?

Chapter Eight

1.   The publication of raw outcomes of schooling reveal very little about the effectiveness of the school.

2. The investigation of 'value' must encompass qualitative as well as quantitative data.

3. School improvement has at its heart the improvement of teaching and learning with effective assessment essential to both.

4. School improvement requires the active involvement of every teacher.

5. Trainee teachers need to encounter the principles of effective assessment not just as something they learn but also something they experience.

One big question:
How do we ensure and monitor excellent
continuing professional development for all
teachers?

Further Reading

Crooks T J (1988) **The Impact of Classroom Evaluation on Students** Review of Educational Research, Vol 5, no 4, pp 438-481

Gipps C V (1990) **Assessment: A Teacher's Guide to the Issues** Hodder and Stoughton

Gipps C V (1994) **Beyond Assessment, Towards a Theory of Educational Assessment** Falmer Press

Satterley D (1989) **Assessment in Schools** (2nd edition) Blackwell

Sutton R (1991) **Assessment: A Framework for Teachers** Routledge